FREE TO LEARN

FREE TO LEARN

LESSONS FROM MODEL CHARTER SCHOOLS

LANCE T. IZUMI AND
XIAOCHIN CLAIRE YAN

PACIFIC
RESEARCH
INSTITUTE

ISBN 0-936488-95-6

Library of Congress Catalog-in-Publication Data

Published in the United States by
Pacific Research Institute
755 Sansome Street, Suite 450
San Francisco, CA 94111
Tel: 415.989.0833 | 800.276.7600
Fax: 415.989.2411
Email: info@pacificresearch.org

Manufactured in the United States of America

10 9 8 7 6 5 4 3 2 1

Additional copies of this book may be purchased by contacting PRI at the address above or at www.pacificresearch.org.

To our parents, who taught us the important lessons

ACKNOWLEDGMENTS

Our gratitude goes out to the charter school principals who took time out of their busy day to walk us through their campuses, introduce us to their staff, and answer our questions. We applaud their amazing work and thank them for their patience.

This book would not have been possible without the generous assistance of many different people and the financial support of several foundations including the Bernard Lee Schwartz Foundation, Inc., Koret Foundation Funds, and the Pisces Foundation.

Gary Larson, Collin Miller, Bill Redford, and Candice Lamarche at the California Charter School Association provided guidance and valuable data to begin our research.

We would like to thank Megan Farnsworth for her work in tailoring the surveys that were sent out to charter school principals and for tabulating the survey results. We would also like to thank Sheila Byrd for peer reviewing the survey instrument.

We would also like to acknowledge the late John Walton for his dedication and commitment to parental choice and his longstanding support for the education work of the Pacific Research Institute.

This book benefited from the counsel and assistance of the dedicated people at the Pacific Research Institute: Rowena Itchon, vice president of marketing and Susan Martin, marketing manager for PRI; Lloyd Billingsley, editorial director; Mary Anne Hanis and Denise Tsui, graphic designers; Lisa Mac Lellan, senior vice president; and Sally C. Pipes, president and CEO of PRI.

TABLE OF CONTENTS

FOREWORD

Charter schools are using their freedom and flexibility to foster new, innovative cultures of student achievement. While charters may have diverse instructional and organizational models, they are focused on improving the performance of their students.

Further, charter schools overall are demonstrating operational accountability. Charter schools are public entities, so they must be responsible with public tax dollars. This means that leaders of charter schools need to be good managers in addition to being educational innovators. Occasionally, good intentions and noble ideas are not enough.

Given this reality, understanding why many charter schools do well, while some struggle, is crucial. In this book, Lance Izumi and Xiaochin Claire Yan of the Pacific Research Institute provide an in-depth look at the educational and organizational models used by successful charter schools. It is not surprising that the schools they profile have a range of philosophies and strategies. However, their finding of common emphases on high student achievement, academic standards, teacher quality, assessment, and management accountability is critical. Charter school operators and consumers would benefit from using these successful models as guides when starting, running or choosing a charter.

Izumi and Yan also do a service to the charter school movement by examining ineffective practices of underachieving charters. Knowing what should be avoided is just as important as knowing what should be emulated.

Charter schools are improving student achievement and transforming the educational landscape. For this positive change to continue and spread, the charter school movement will continue to stress quality. The enlightening information contained in this book will help to ensure that charter schools committed to high-quality will meet the challenge of positively impacting the broader public school system in the years ahead.

Caprice Young
President and CEO, California Charter School Association
Former President, Los Angeles Unified School District Board of Education

INTRODUCTION

On March 6, 1999, 17-year-old Francisco was shot dead on his driveway, apparently a victim of gang rivalry. His home was just a block from Vaughn Street Elementary School where he graduated in 1993. Today, his younger brother, Eddie, a fourth grader at the same school, is a member of the student council and determined to go to college.

What changed? When Francisco attended Vaughn, the school offered only 163 days of instruction and students were split on a three-track schedule due to overcrowding. Counseling and after-school tutoring were not available. Francisco was bused briefly to another school for four months due to a court-ordered desegregation plan.

As soon as he was identified as a severely learning-disabled student, he was then bused to another district school because Vaughn did not provide special education services. He was only able to come back to Vaughn when his parents waived the right to intensive special education services in the fourth grade. Chronic asthma prevented him from maintaining regular attendance. The school could do nothing to help Francisco.

Vaughn converted to a public charter school in 1993. Charter schools are deregulated public schools that are given greater freedom and flexibility to innovate in order to achieve better student performance. A year later, Francisco's brother, Eddie, started at the new Vaughn Next Century Learning Center. Eddie gets 200 full days of instruction in addition to daily after-school academic and enrichment programs. Overcrowding is no longer a problem because the new charter school was able to build an additional 56 classrooms.

Eddie's learning disabilities were identified as early as kindergarten, and Vaughn was able to give him the intervention he needed. The school is a full-service stop for all of Eddie's needs: co-teaching by general and special education teachers, speech therapy, peer tutoring, after-school tutoring, family counseling, and even a site-based health clinic operated by the county. Eddie was able to leave the special education program by third grade.

Not only that, Eddie's mother is taking a GED class at Vaughn offered by the district's adult education division. On her way to the Vaughn Family Center where she and other parents volunteer for childcare services, she keeps an eye on the new construction site where a high school annex is being built. When Eddie graduates from elementary school, he will be able to stay for middle school and high school.

As a traditional public school, Vaughn failed to help Francisco. As a charter school, it has provided his brother with unlimited opportunities and a world-class education. Located in Pacoima, California, a high-poverty and high-crime area, Vaughn serves the same mostly low-income minority kids, many of whom are English learners and have special education needs, that it used to misserve 15 years ago. The student demographics have not changed, but the school has — thanks to its new charter status flexibilities and the boundless energy and resourcefulness of principal Yvonne Chan.

Unfortunately, not all the news one hears about charter schools is positive. There has been a great deal of debate over how charter schools compare with traditional public schools. The *New York Times* gave wide coverage to a study of charter schools by the American Federation of Teachers, reporting that "charter school students often do worse than comparable students in regular public schools." Critics rightly point out that such studies are often based on one-year snapshots of data and do not show how much charter schools may be improving over time.

Are there bad charter schools out there? Absolutely. (Later in this book, successful charter school principals are asked why some charters don't make the cut.) But that charter schools can and do fail is one of their most important features. Unlike traditional public schools, where low student achievement and ineffective teaching methods often go uncorrected for decades, charters must show results to stay open and attract students. If they don't, they will go out of business.

This allowance for failure ensures that only the better quality schools survive, benefiting students and parents. Howard Lappin, one of the charter school principals interviewed for this book, observed, "A few more people failing and a few more people getting kicked out would be a good thing."

Charters are by nature different not just from traditional public schools, but from one another. With their freedom and flexibility, many charter schools have made great strides in improving the achievement of previously low-performing students. Schools like Vaughn have opened doors and opportunities that many poor and minority children, who are still trapped at failing campuses run by district bureaucracies, will never glimpse.

During the research and writing of this book, we witnessed innovative and principled educators making full and wise use of their charter freedoms. In the tough inner-city neighborhoods of Oakland, we met principal Ben Chavis, whose unconventional methods have catapulted his charter school into the lofty position of the highest performing middle school in the district. In South Sacramento, we found Dennis Mah, another charter principal with a dramatic turnaround story. He took a school where students were literally climbing out of classroom windows and built it into one where students embrace learning and score high on state tests.

How did they do it? What these successful charter principals and teachers are doing often runs completely contrary to the conventional wisdom of the public education establishment. The highly improving schools profiled in this book have perfected alternative models of organization, management, teaching, and discipline that shatter the status quo orthodoxy.

Lawmakers and educators need to realize what can be accomplished when educational freedom is used wisely as the means to achieve high student performance. It won't be easy. The powerful special-interest players in the public school system are hugely resistant to real change. However, with state and federal accountability systems forcing schools to raise student achievement, the time is coming when regular public schools must start to emulate their successful charter brethren.

The Pacific Research Institute has been a longtime supporter of increased parental choice options in education. Charter schools are an important option, which is why it is critical for parents and others to learn and understand what makes for a good charter school. Once it is known which models work, then these models can be replicated. California governor Arnold Schwarzenegger has praised successful charter schools, saying:

> Charter schools are pathfinders in education reform. They help parents and educators tailor programs to fit their community's needs. They also allow greater teaching and financial flexibility and centralize decision-making at the local level. These schools serve more of our low-income and minority students and provide focused help for students who struggle academically. They put student needs first, and their approach is working.

The highly improving charter schools profiled in this book have these characteristics. We have written this book to share its success stories so that other charters can study and follow their example.

The first seven chapters of *Free to Learn* profile continuously highly performing charter schools. Each of these schools exceeded its state test-score growth targets for three consecutive years from 2001–02 to 2003–04.

While it is important to understand why some charter schools do so well, it is equally necessary to examine why others are so ineffective. In chapter eight, we ask successful charter principals to discuss the reasons some charter schools fail to make the grade.

The next two chapters profile two charter schools very different from the previous seven. One tells why statistics are sometimes deceptive and the other shows the difficulties facing a struggling charter. Finally, we draw conclusions on what makes for an effective or ineffective charter model.

In the years we have been studying education reform, and in the time we have come to know these particular schools and their principals, we believe charter schools are capable of great things. In California and in the nation today, too few schools are thinking outside the box. The chief reason charter schools are successful is very simple: freedom. Schools are free from micro-managing districts and meddling politicians. Principals are free to be leaders, not mid-level bureaucrats. Teachers are free to practice as professionals. Most important, at a good charter school, students are free to learn.

Parents' Guide to Effective and Ineffective Charter Schools

Parents should look for charter schools that:

- ✔ Maintain good management and consistent stable, leadership — focusing on student achievement, cost efficiency, and fiscal accountability

- ✔ Emphasize academic rather than non-academic goals, with high expectations for students and staff

- ✔ Implement rigorous standards-based curricula

- ✔ Hire smart teachers based on top academic records — rather than relying simply on possession of a regular teaching credential

- ✔ Create grade-level teams of teachers to analyze student data, plan for interventions, and design instruction

- ✔ Test students often and use results as diagnostic tools to spot weaknesses

- ✔ Prevent grade inflation by comparing grades with test scores

- ✔ Use teaching methods that are empirically proven to improve student performance

- ✔ Ensure classroom accountability through frequent classroom visits by the principal

- ✔ Promote high-quality teaching through rigorous teacher evaluations, with tough consequences for poor performance

Parents should avoid charter schools that:

✗ Are wracked by infighting among organizers, board members, administrators, staff, and parents

✗ Go through multiple principals over a short period of time, thus failing to give the school stable, consistent leadership

✗ Deprive the principal of decision-making authority through micromanagement by the governing board

✗ Are fiscally inefficient and irresponsible due to lack of management and business experience on the part of school leaders

✗ Focus on the non-academic ideals of adults at the school rather than on the academic needs and achievement of students

✗ Use unrealistic and/or unproven philosophies of teaching or learning

✗ Fail to use charter freedoms and flexibilities to break the status quo public school mold

✗ De-emphasize student testing and the importance of the state's rigorous academic content standards

✗ Hold back perceived low-performing students from taking the state's standardized tests

✗ Promote weak curricula, with no textbooks provided to students

CHAPTER ONE

BEATING THOSE GUYS IN PIEDMONT

I take these kids to all these events, to math competitions, and I say that those white kids over there say they're going to whip your a**. . .

— BEN CHAVIS, PRINCIPAL

American Indian Public Charter School, Grades 6–8
Oakland, California

IT IS VERY DIFFICULT FOR CHILDREN, especially those from low socioeconomic backgrounds, to get a good education in Oakland. The city's school district has been in fiscal disarray, student achievement has been poor at many schools, and safety and discipline issues are constant concerns. There are few bright spots in this bleak educational landscape, which is why the American Indian Public Charter School stands out like a beacon.

Located in a tough inner-city neighborhood in the so-called Oakland "flatland," American Indian occupies a nondescript multi-story building that has been leased from a church next door. One could easily drive or walk past the campus without realizing that it was a school or, more important, that an educational miracle was occurring within its walls. It is the highest-performing middle school in Oakland. Walk up a flight of stairs to the school's small administrative office and one meets Dr. Ben Chavis, the principal of American Indian and the man primarily responsible for the school's amazing success.

Lean, handsome, and middle-aged, with short graying hair, a stylish goatee, a glint in his eye, and a huge personality, Ben Chavis is a most

---

The Model

▶ Self-contained classrooms where students are taught every subject by the same teacher for three consecutive years

▶ Smart teachers hired on their top academic records, and not simply because they possess regular teaching credentials

▶ Use of charter flexibility to pay teachers significantly more than school district salary

▶ Collaborative professional development with teachers training their colleagues

▶ High goals for the school and high expectations for the students and staff

▶ Rigorous standards-based curricula. Two sets of standards-aligned textbooks for students, one for class use and one for use at home

▶ Test scores used as diagnostic tools

▶ Use of monetary incentives to encourage perfect student attendance

▶ Good management leadership focusing on cost efficiency and fiscal responsibility

---

memorable person. A former school superintendent at an Indian reservation in Arizona, Chavis is an Indian himself and a businessman who owns various rental properties. He was one of 10 children, with a single mother who worked as a maid.

Combining a keen understanding of what works in education with street smarts, business acumen, and a fearless animosity toward political correctness, Chavis is a goal-driven leader who has high expectations for his students, his staff, and himself. How high? "I'm a dictator," he said. "You need a dictator sometimes. I like to fire people. I'm not the type that feels sorry for you, because I have a goal. You are on my team or you're not."

Goals are extremely important to Chavis:

> You got to have goals. When I came here we were the worst school in the city. My goal was to improve the first year. After that, my second year I said we were going to be the best middle school. Every year you have to have a goal. But I'm never going to be happy until I beat those guys in Piedmont [the affluent suburb in the hills outside Oakland]. I take these kids to all these events, to math competitions, and I say that those white kids over there say they're going to whip your a**. . . . We'll go to events where we're the only public school from Oakland. [The private schools] will then give scholarships to my kids to go to high school.

Indeed, annually an eyebrow-raising number of American Indian's students are selected for Johns Hopkins University's nationally noted talent search program. Out of the 16 American Indian seventh graders who took the test to enter the program, an amazing 15 qualified.

Chavis's tough leadership style was sorely needed by the time American Indian recruited him to head the school. Chartered in 1996, American Indian had floundered academically. When its charter was up for renewal, it was very likely that the Oakland school board would withdraw the charter and close the school. Several poorly performing charter schools had had their charters revoked the same year that American Indian's was up for renewal. Rather than trying to defend a poor record, as the other

2003–04 Demographics

Hispanic	28%
African American	24%
American Indian	22%
Asian	21%
English language learners	42%

Academic Performance Index (API) Growth Comparisons

2001	2002	2003	2004
436 454	572 606	722 735	816

■ Base Score ■ Growth Target ■ Growth

failing charters had done, Chavis admitted the school's problems and asked for the chance to put things right and set the school on a course toward achievement. The school board decided to give Chavis a shot.

Using the freedom that charters have in personnel policy, Chavis said: "I got rid of the whole staff. I got rid of every last one of them." A new governance board was put in place with members drawn from varied professional backgrounds.

Chavis then started to rebuild the school from scratch. He had to hire high-quality teachers. He had to develop a successful educational model and create an achievement-oriented academic culture. He also had to use his funds wisely because American Indian was getting less money than standard public schools. When searching for new teachers, Chavis turned to an unusual source — Craigslist.com, a website featuring free classified advertisements and forums by topic: "Think about this. Who are the people on Craigslist? Young, smart people." During recruitment, Chavis said:

> First thing I ask for is a copy of their resume and then their transcripts. . . . All these guys are smart. You look at a smart person in philosophy or sociology or mathematics, they're smart overall. People say that doesn't mean you're going to be a good teacher. That's true, but I meet them and visit with them and I think I have a pretty good instinct for good people. I make mistakes, but when I make them they don't last too long.

Teachers at American Indian, therefore, have impressive backgrounds. We observed one sixth-grade classroom that was taught by a teacher with an undergraduate degree from Columbia University, a law degree from Georgetown University, and five years of experience as a working attorney. Not exactly the profile of the average teacher in Oakland.

One thing that Chavis was not looking for in a new teacher was a regular teaching credential from a state university: "That's a minus. You think I'm joking? I'm serious." "A credential," emphasizes Chavis, "doesn't equal quality." He believes that the pedagogies taught by university schools of education are ineffective: "The problem is that they're all b-s, to be honest with you." Schools of education, Chavis believes, do not place enough importance on content instruction:

They spend too much time on methodology and not content. You can
teach with 16 units of math and 50 units of methodology. Seems like a
problem to me . . . . You've got to know content, the reading, the math.
In colleges of education, think about it, how many professors of education know anything about math? Science? They know methodology.

"I've come to the conclusion," he said, "that whatever a college of
education says or whatever people say we should do in education, I do
the opposite." During his time at American Indian, he has hired only one
fully credentialed teacher.

How does American Indian attract smart young people? First, by using
charter flexibility to put the school's limited resources into paying teachers
more than the union-negotiated salaries in the Oakland school district.
American Indian's starting teacher salary of $42,000 is around $5,000 more
than the starting salary in the district. Chavis recalled, "The president of the
union said to me, 'Ben, we haven't figured out how not to upset our teachers
if we take your people because you're paying more.'" American Indian's
teachers, thus, are non-union, in part because the union will not let the
school's higher-paid teachers join lest they disrupt the uniform salary
structure negotiated by the union with the district.

Further, American Indian pays a variety of bonuses to teachers, such
as a Christmas bonus and a $500 bonus for perfect attendance. The
school also gives out a schoolwide performance bonus that is partly
based on improvement of student test scores. The performance bonus
goes to support staff and teachers.

Chavis is constantly going into the classrooms to see how students
are progressing. He said: "I've never evaluated a teacher here — what
you would call a written evaluation — but I go into the classroom three
or four times a day. But I'm not going in to evaluate, I'm going in to
check on the kids." Because his hiring criteria emphasizes intelligence
and accomplishment, he said that his classroom observations tell him
how his teachers are doing: "First of all, these teachers here are extraordinary. I hired them, I know them. These are good people. You can tell
by their lesson plans, by what they're doing in class, what the kids are
engaged in. So that's the evaluation."

"You have to have goals. When I came here we were the worst school in the city. My goal was to improve the first year. After that, my second year I said we were going to be the best middle school. Every year you have to have a goal. But I'm never going to be happy until I beat those guys in Piedmont."

Having excellent teachers is tremendously important, as research shows that teacher quality is one of the most significant factors impacting student achievement. Yet the way schools use good teachers is also critical. Chavis addressed this issue by creating an innovative educational model. Instead of the usual middle school routine of students moving from one subject to another with each class taught by a different teacher, Chavis changed to a self-contained classroom model where teachers teach all subjects and move with their students from one grade to the next. Thus, a teacher begins with a class of students in the sixth grade, goes with them through the eighth grade, and after the class graduates he or she starts all over again with a new sixth-grade class. Since students will be with the same teacher every day for their entire middle school career, it becomes obvious why Chavis emphasizes getting high-quality teachers in the classroom.

Teacher professional development is based on the self-contained classroom model. "What we do," said Chavis, "is when you're teaching the sixth grade and move up to the seventh, the new sixth-grade teacher is coming in, you're going to train him or her and the teacher who is in the seventh grade is going to train you." Chavis observed that this type of collaborative professional development has worked well at the school: "If you taught in the sixth grade, they're going to say this is the part of the book you really need to focus on or I found this difficult for the kids. So they're training the teachers."

Chavis stated bluntly, "We use our own people to train," and "I don't have consultants." He pointed to one poorly performing charter school in Oakland, saying that the principal has coaches. Low-performing traditional public schools in Oakland also have coaches for the principal. Chavis asked, "Why don't you just fire the principal and hire the coach?" He also pointed out that these coaches and consultants in Oakland "will go all over the area to visit good middle schools, but they never come to visit us."

The self-contained classroom model also saves the school a lot of money. Fewer staff persons are needed. Fewer facilities are needed because the students are not rotating. Rotation also wears out facilities faster. Even more important than saving dollars, however, is the effect that the model has on building an esprit de corps among students and teachers. As Chavis noted:

> Remember, this is a family. These are little clans. They've spent three years together. [They start in sixth grade] and move with the teacher to the seventh grade. When they get to the eighth grade and they graduate, the teacher goes on a trip with them. They spend a week in Washington, D.C., then they come back.

This "extended family" concept is one of the keys to American Indian's stable learning environment and its ability to maintain discipline among students. The students bond and help each other academically and encourage one another to behave. A charter-school publication quotes Sally Mitchell, a Sioux Indian student at the school:

> In elementary school, I missed over 50 days of school some years. I would fall asleep in class. I didn't pay attention. At this school, we are like a family. We work through things because we care for each other. I'm working hard to keep my grades up. Miss Houseman (her teacher) makes sure that everyone in our class is learning. This is why we are the top middle school in Oakland.

Chavis uses the "extended family" concept in unusual ways. Thus, when a student behaves badly, he calls aunts, uncles, and grandparents. With a grin, he said, "I'm big on embarrassment."

High-quality teachers in self-contained classrooms still need good tools. Chavis has given his teachers these tools in the form of the state academic content standards, good textbooks, and a solid curriculum. Of the state standards, he said, "They're number one." When asked how he turned around the academic program at American Indian, he advised: "Get textbooks. I'm a big believer in textbooks. That's another thing that your lousy performing schools have in common, they're not using textbooks." He notes that his school was the first in Oakland to get textbooks aligned with the state academic content standards.

Further, he said that students have to be able to take those textbooks home with them in order to study and learn. He criticized poorly performing charter schools for not allowing students to take home textbooks and only maintaining a set for classroom use. At American Indian, children have two sets of textbooks, one for the classroom and another for use at home.

In an interesting departure from conventional wisdom, Chavis opposes the use of computers in the classroom. He said that children from the area, who do not want to work hard, will break the computer in order to avoid assignments.

The coursework at American Indian is difficult. The school is one of only two in Oakland where every eighth-grader is taking algebra. Even special education students at the school take algebra in the eighth grade. "In the [regular] public schools," said Chavis, "[minorities] are getting remedial math, algebra is only for the Asians and the wealthy whites." His students take algebra "because I demand it." He said, "I have high expectations. I don't need excuses. I don't care if you're special ed, it doesn't matter. You sit and practice, guys, practice."

In addition to math, time for English/language arts is sacred. Chavis said: "From 8:30 a.m. until 10 a.m. is language arts, nothing can interrupt this. Language arts is the foundation. If

Instead of the usual middle school routine of students moving from one subject to another with each class taught by a different teacher, Chavis changed to a self-contained classroom model where teachers teach all subjects and move with their students from one grade to the next.

you've got to go to the doctor, you better schedule it after 10 a.m."

American Indian's high expectations for its all-minority student body can be attributed in part to Chavis's philosophy about race. He said, "When I ran track, I didn't get a head start because I was Indian." All students, no matter their ethnicity, start at the same place. When he worked at the University of Arizona, he refused to put his race on applications, and was placed on business committees rather than affirmative action committees. That result suited him just fine since he opposes race preferences. "I don't care what color you are," he said.

When asked how he turned around the academic program at American Indian, he advised: "Get textbooks. I'm a big believer in textbooks."

Teachers at American Indian use a teacher-centered lecture-style method of instruction. Teachers' lesson plans are very detailed so that Chavis knows what the teacher is doing in every class, every day, in every subject. And, again, he said practice works and his students are constantly practicing the knowledge and skills they are being taught. He pointed out: "My Title I funds go to two things: books and teacher salaries. What we're doing is so simple. All this stuff about [educating] the 'whole child,' the 'global citizen,' how are you going to measure that?"

State tests and student scores are important diagnostic tools at American Indian. When test data comes out in the summer, Chavis pores over the results. He looks at his students who did not do well, those scoring far below or below the basic level, and targets them. Supplemental instruction, often after school, is given to these struggling students. Chavis also does not hide the fact that he prepares his students for the tests:

> When you run track, just before the state championship or the nationals, you get sharp, you cut down on your distance and do some short distance and get your speed ready. Testing is the same way. We've been doing math all year, now we're going to focus down — here are some key things you need to know. That's what really helps our kids. The kids know that we always emphasize being the best. What does being the best mean? It means doing your best.

Chavis said that in 2004 every child, with one exception, improved his or her test performance. He has words of wisdom for parents who may not like student testing:

> Parents and kids need to be educated as to why these tests are important. I find a lot of the kids that come here didn't know. It wasn't that they couldn't do it. I met a parent the other day who applied and she said that her kid doesn't take tests, she said that they discriminate. So I said I wonder how that test is going to figure out you're Jamaican? So I said how is your kid going to get into Berkeley? They've got to take a test. So go ahead, don't offer them any more tests, wait until they have to take the college entrance exam, and they're going to be freaking out.

Testing is part of American Indian's overall emphasis on accountability, which includes meeting and exceeding the goals of the federal No Child Left Behind Act (NCLB). Again, swimming against the conventional education current, Chavis fearlessly proclaimed, "I believe as a minority parent and educator, NCLB is the greatest educational policy created by any branch of the United States government for minority students in the past hundred years." "For the first time," he continued, "public schools are held accountable for providing minority and poor students with the proficient academic skills needed to compete in our democratic society."

One thing that Chavis said is not the key to better student achievement is money. He observed provocatively: "Money's not the answer. Schools have too much money." His school runs in the black, unlike the Oakland school district, even though it receives less money than a district school. His federal Title I dollars go only to books and teacher salaries. He does not apply for private grants because he does not want the strings that may be attached to those grants. Schools, he said, can

"I believe as a minority parent and educator, NCLB is the greatest educational policy created by any branch of the United States government for minority students in the past hundred years."

do well if they manage their dollars better: "We don't need more money, we need administrators who can manage money."

American Indian uses its money in many creative ways. For example, the school rewards sixth graders for perfect attendance by giving them $50 at the end of the year. Seventh graders receive $75 and eighth graders receive $100 for not missing a day of class. Three years of perfect attendance are rewarded with a $150 bonus. Not surprisingly, students have responded to these incentives. More than 80 percent of eighth graders have not missed a day of class in three years. The school's average daily attendance rate is 99.67 percent. As Chavis pointed out: "I'm teaching them to be capitalists. These [bad] guys in their neighborhoods say, 'Hey man, if you fill this bag of weed, I'll give you $5.' The kids say, 'If I go to school every day I'm going to get $50 or $100.'"

> As Chavis pointed out:
> "I'm teaching them to be capitalists. These [bad] guys in their neighborhoods say, 'Hey man, if you fill this bag of weed, I'll give you $5.' The kids say, 'If I go to school every day I'm going to get $50 or $100.'"

Chavis will even follow up with students who have moved to a different school and still reward them if they continue to maintain perfect attendance. Chavis is serious about the importance of teaching the principles of capitalism to his students:

> [Minority children] come from the 'hood and they see drug dealers and all these things. And I tell them, you know what I'm going to teach you? I'm going to teach you how to take the big man's money legally without going to jail. The kids come here saying I want to play for the Raiders or I want to play for the Lakers. No, you want to own them. You want to be a businessperson. If you want to be in charge of your life, you've got to own some kind of property.

Once at school, students are required to be on their very best behavior. The school enforces a strict zero-tolerance discipline code. Chavis said:

"You get detention if you're one second late, if you look at the teacher wrong. Kids are not equal to teachers. I'm not equal to George Bush. We are not into tolerance. I don't tolerate fools."

Chavis observed that one can judge how good a school or school system is by whether teachers, principals, and district officials are willing to enroll their own children. It turns out that the Oakland public schools are not good enough for many children of educators. Chavis pointed out:

> The county superintendent of public instruction in Alameda sends her kid to [a private school] but then she says that charter schools are undermining public schools. . . . She sends her kid to a private school but I'm the one undermining public schools! Now she's the county superintendent. She doesn't have any place in the public schools. Now look at the number of teachers who are sending their kids to charter schools. Teachers know where the best schools are. I've got two principals who want to get their kids in. . . . Here's my question. If [teachers] don't believe in testing, why do they look at the tests and bring their kids over here?

Finally, Ben Chavis posts a set of 16 rules on the door of his office. Titled "Common Sense & Useful Learning at American Indian Public Charter School," the rules are an intoxicating breath of fresh air that wither the weeds of received wisdom promulgated by the public education establishment.

- The school facility is open daily from 8:30 a.m. until 4 p.m., except Saturdays, Sundays, and all holidays known to mankind.

- The staff of AIPCS does not preach or subscribe to the demagoguery of tolerance. Anyone who does not follow our rules will be sent packing with their rags and bags!

- Squawkers, multicultural specialists, self-esteem experts, panhandlers, drug dealers, and those snapping turtles who refuse to put forth their best effort will be booted out.

- Boot licking or self promoting is not allowed by any politician who enters our classrooms. Politicians should beware, teachers are on duty.

- We do not believe that standardized tests discriminate against students because of their color. Could it be many of them have not been adequately prepared to take those tests?

- The staff does not allow students to wear hats, gold chains, or ear bobs in the building. Adults are not allowed to use cell phones, beepers, and other gadgets in our school.

- Dr. Chavis does provide psychological evaluations to quacks and Kultur specialists on a sliding scale. See him immediately for such rates.

- All solicitors should note the nearest exit upon entering this institution of learning. We view such alley cats with a fishy eye.

- No more than one psychologist or school administrator is allowed in our school at a time. This is part of our commitment to high academic standards.

- Photographs of the Director and Staff are on sale at the front office. Payment must be made in advance. CASH ONLY! The photographs will be sent to you by pony express.

- The staff of AIPCS are of the first rank. We request that you do not flirt with them. They will accept your cash donations!

- Visitors are welcome daily. Due to the time it takes to reeducate university visitors, we are limiting their number to a maximum of four individuals a week.

- It will be difficult for our staff to meet with those educational experts who "know it all." We are willing to meet with such tom cats on Halloween night.

- How does anyone convince a billy goat or taxpayer that school administrators possess above-average intelligence? How will we address this educational dilemma?

- Our staff does not subscribe to the back swamp logic of minority students as victims. We will plow through such cornfield philosophy with common sense and hard work!

- If you wish to share any suggestions regarding this page, our common sense committee accepts suggestions from 8:30 a.m. to 8:31 a.m. each holiday.

CHAPTER TWO

NO BLAME GAME

We can't blame it on parents. We can't blame it on the socioeconomic background of kids. We can't blame it on parent education or English language deficiencies. We have to take responsibility and be accountable for what happens here.

— LINDA MIKELS, PRINCIPAL

Sixth Street Prep, Grades K–6
Victorville, California

DRIVE TWO HOURS EAST OF LOS ANGELES into the California desert and one comes upon the town of Victorville. Small and unassuming, Victorville is nonetheless home to a jewel of a charter school. Located in very modest quarters near the local school district headquarters, Sixth Street Prep charter school is not the easiest place to find. But the hunt is well worth it, in view of the success the school's low-income, mostly Hispanic students are having in the classroom.

Sixth Street is an oasis of hope in a troubled neighborhood. Vandalism is a constant problem. Also, the school shares its playground with a local city park. Syringes left by drug addicts must be swept daily off the asphalt. Yet despite the difficult environment, learning has taken a strong hold at the school.

Sixth Street's principal is Linda Mikels, a focused, no-nonsense woman with clear ideas about what works and what doesn't when it comes to raising student achievement. In her fourth year as the school's leader, this assignment is her first as principal. She had served as director of instruction

---

The Model

▸ Focus initially on math achievement for mostly English-language-learner student population

▸ Repeated practice through a system of "mini-skills" assessments, review of assessments, and a 10-question review of previously learned skills that students must do every morning

▸ Curricula, such as Mountain Math, emphasize "spiral review" that continuously reinforces skills that have been previously taught

▸ A structured, direct instruction teaching methodology

▸ Test scores influence design of instruction and types of interventions

▸ Regular meetings of grade-level teachers to score student writing, score other student assessments, plan for interventions, and design instruction

▸ Staff development influenced by Ruby Payne, a well-known authority on the effect of poverty on children's learning behavior

---

at the district office in Apple Valley. While working as a district administrator, she became convinced that she could make a bigger difference and a more significant contribution at a school site than in the district office.

She took a position as assistant principal in neighboring Rialto and discovered some of her leadership gifts, abilities, and passions. These attributes also became apparent to others, and when Sixth Street Prep was chartered, a number of local principals urged her to take over the top spot at the school. She agreed.

A conversion charter school, Sixth Street had originally been a K–3 primary school. Mikels said that parents wanted to keep their children in the school until the sixth grade. To accomplish this goal, they had to lease back from the city the nearby old town council building, built in 1922, and use it as a school. Since the building did not meet Field Act earthquake standards for regular public schools, the only way to use the building was to gain an exemption from the law's requirements by becoming a charter school.

While facility needs may have spurred the move to convert Sixth Street into a charter, the school was also going through some dramatic demographic and academic changes. The school had become overwhelmingly Hispanic and many students did not speak English fluently. The socioeconomic background of the students changed as well, with large numbers of students living in poverty. Most disturbing, student test scores were nose-diving.

Against this challenging back-drop, Linda Mikels threw down an educational gauntlet. In one of her first meetings with her teachers after assuming the leadership role, Mikels shared the test score data with teachers and recalled telling them:

2003–04 Demographics	
Hispanic	77%
White	14%
African American	7%
English language learners	49%
Free and reduced lunch	90%

Academic Performance Index (API) Growth Comparisons

	2001	2002	2003	2004
	599	609 625	640 688	696 728

Base Score Growth Target Growth

> We have to agree together to have a no-excuses environment here. We can't blame it on parents. We can't blame it on the socioeconomic background of kids. We can't blame it on parent education or English language deficiencies. We have to take responsibility and be accountable for what happens here. From day one I felt a unity that we would not make excuses.

Mikels also mentioned that Sixth Street's previous principal was focused on brain research, which seeks to explain how people learn. So-called "brain-based learning" usually involves designing a curriculum around student interests, using real-world problems as the basis for

> Mikels brought with her a philosophy that emphasized the importance of practice. She observes that a concept "is never fully learned without many, many repeated opportunities for practice."

instruction, and allowing students to monitor and assess themselves. Supporters of brain-based learning believe that feedback is best when it comes from "reality" rather than an authority figure such as a teacher.

All the staff development at Sixth Street was based around brain research. Mikels allowed that perhaps this brain research focus may have had some merit, but she was interested in what good instruction looked like, and it simply was not happening at the school when she arrived.

After examining student test score data, Mikels and her teachers decided to focus on one problem at a time. Improving math achievement became their first goal because, said Mikels, she wanted students "to see immediate success, and you can see success with an English language learner in the area of math." She acknowledges that some outside the school disagreed with the focus on math, believing that reading/language arts should have been the first priority. Yet the math focus remained. The school uses Houghton-Mifflin's standards-aligned math textbooks, which the district has adopted, but supplements them with the cumulative assessments found in the Scott-Forsman math curriculum.

Mikels brought with her a philosophy that emphasized the importance of practice. She observes that a concept "is never fully learned without many, many repeated opportunities for practice." She and her staff created a system in which students were assessed on small sets of skills called "mini-skills." The teachers would go over these assessments and there would be constant re-teaching of these skills, which would involve a skill objective for each day. Mikels and her teachers worked together to assemble 10-question reviews of previously learned skills that students must do every morning.

In conjunction with these reviews, students use high-tech tools such as infrared input devices that create graphs to allow teachers to instantly see a student's response to a question and determine where re-teaching needs to take place. The assessment drives the classroom instruction.

Sixth Street also uses review programs such as Mountain Math, which assigns students daily review problems. Such programs emphasize so-called "spiral review" that continuously reinforces skills that have been previously taught. Mikels observes that spiral review is common sense, pointing out that unless adults had been practicing their math skills they would not be able to do math problems from their last high school or college math course. Given this reality, "Well, why would our children be any different?" This review and practice strategy, she believes, is the "primary reason for phenomenal math growth over the last four years."

In insisting that practice makes perfect, Mikels is on solid empirical grounds. University of Illinois education researchers Barak Rosenshine and Robert Stevens found that in order to process and transfer new information from working memory to long-term memory, people have to "elaborate, review, rehearse, summarize, or enhance the material." Therefore, teachers "should provide active practice for all students." Material should, in essence, be overlearned because "there is value in repeating and rehearsing basic material that will be used in subsequent learning." A key fact, say Rosenshine and Stevens, is that:

> [N]ew learning is easier when prior learning is readily accessible or automatic. In a large number of academic situations the student needs to apply and use the knowledge and skills that have been previously learned. Retention and application of previously learned knowledge and skills comes through overlearning, that is, practice beyond the point where the student has to work to give the correct response. This results in automatic processes which are rapidly executed and require little or no conscious attention. When prior learning is automatic, space is freed in our working memory, which can be used for comprehension, application, and problem solving.

Further, the California mathematics framework, adopted by the state in 1998, emphasizes that "students must practice skills in order to become proficient." The framework says that practice and memorization of arithmetic facts are important because "the ability to retrieve these facts automatically from long-term memory, in turn, makes the solving of more complex problems, such as multi-step problems that involve basic arithmetic, quicker and less likely to result in error."

Even with practice, what about the fact that students learn at different paces? This seeming conundrum is solved by the mini-lessons/mini-assessments/spiral review. Mikels said:

> So we believe that not all students learn the same objectives at the same time. So if that's the case, if you're teaching a unit right now on multiplication, we would say that you don't keep that student there who's not getting it until they get it. You keep moving them on knowing that two or three times a week they are going to continue to get mini-lessons and it might not be until you get down to figuring the area of a rectangle that it starts to click with them and starts to make sense.

Teachers at Sixth Street use a structured direct instruction teaching method. Under direct instruction, teachers explain exactly what students are expected to learn and demonstrate the steps needed to accomplish a particular academic task. Direct instruction is usually characterized by: 1) setting clear goals for students and making sure students understand the goals, 2) presenting a sequence of well-organized assignments, 3) giving students clear, concise explanations and illustrations of the subject matter, 4) asking frequent questions to see if students understand the material, and 5) giving students frequent opportunities to practice what they have learned.

Mikels said that direct instruction was adopted because of the research that supports its effectiveness in raising student achievement, especially among low-socioeconomic students. Indeed, a wide range of studies by the federal government and university and independent researchers have found that direction instruction teaching methods are effective in improving student achievement.

Mikels does not use direct instruction techniques exclusively, but she said that she is extremely careful to ensure that her students have strong background knowledge before any other techniques are used. Without this background knowledge, children end up getting confused. This confusion leads not only to poor performance, but bad attitudes toward the entire learning process.

To facilitate the direct instruction approach, Sixth Street teachers make extensive use of PowerPoint. "A lot of our lessons," said Mikels, "are aided by visuals with PowerPoint as teachers go through and do the direct instruction, even the checking for understanding."

With the school's students achieving admirable results in math, Mikels said that the focus is now turning to reading and writing. She noted, "One of the things that we decided our students needed a lot more of that we were not doing as much as we should is teacher-modeled reading — read-alouds by the teacher all the way through grade six."

At Sixth Street, teachers model reading, comprehension strategies, and vocabulary strategies, and then students use the model in reading books from a classroom library. "It's highly structured," according to Mikels, "in terms of scripted [material] for the teacher and it always brings in a [literary] character development piece because students have to interact with each other about characters and setting and so on, and then they come back and share with the class what they discussed."

In addition to regular reading instruction during the school day, Sixth Street also uses reading intervention and after-school programs. Said Mikels, "Primarily what we do is interventions in reading, one-

Mikels said that direct instruction was adopted because of the research that supports its effectiveness in raising student achievement, especially among low-socioeconomic students.

on-one teaching in a small group, and we have a 'making meaning' group that meets after school for building vocabulary and comprehension strategies."

Teaching reading at the school is a challenge because of the large number of English language learners. While the school does have a bilingual aide who works in classrooms and helps with vocabulary building and comprehension strategies, Mikels stressed, "But our primary approach is full [English] immersion." Under English immersion, English grammar and vocabulary instruction is blended with the teaching of subject-matter content. Mikels said that immersion is producing excellent results at her school:

> And generally the good news is that we've had tremendous success with having a student who is brand new from Mexico and you would walk into the classroom 12 months later and you wouldn't be able to pick out which one he was. It's working, it's working for us. We're excited. Our feeling is that if within 12 months that student is going to have to test at grade level, then we believe it's criminal to drag our feet and to even attempt the dual immersion where he's not going to make the kind of growth that he needs to make so as not to feel like a failure when he has to sit down in front of that test.

Mikels believes that the low transition rate to English fluency under bilingual education was a real indictment of the system that existed before the passage of Proposition 227, the ballot measure that virtually eliminated bilingual education in California classrooms. She is also critical of dual immersion, a variation of bilingual education, where instruction is in two languages.

She said, "I have real problems with it because that system starts students at 90 percent native language, 10 percent [English], then 80-20, and then 70-30, and then they're in sixth grade and moving to junior high and what have you done for them?" She noted that research shows that there are windows of opportunity for learning a language and "the window of opportunity for English language acquisition of any kind was really before seven years old." Thus, her goal is "get them as early as we can, and fully immerse them as quickly as we can, because that's when the language learning just comes so much more naturally."

Advocates of bilingual education have tried to convince parents of limited-English-proficient students to sign waivers to opt out of English immersion classes and remain in bilingual classrooms. Mikels, however, said that parents at Sixth Street want their children to learn English as quickly as possible. She said: "We have many parents who speak only Spanish in the home, but they are very supportive. They know that they live in a culture where English is going to be the ticket that is going to help their children either get a higher education or a significant career opportunity, and so they're very supportive."

Many principals at high-poverty, high-performing schools have remarked that they would rather have new or emergency-credentialed teachers than more experienced teachers because the former have fewer biases and are more trainable than veteran teachers. Nancy Ichinaga, the famed former principal and state Board of Education member, hired mostly emergency-credentialed teachers because they had less baggage and were easier to train in her school's direct-instruction methods. Likewise, Linda Mikels said:

> There is one thing I've really been fortunate about, which would probably be looked at by some folks who study low-performing schools as the reason for low performance, but which I consider a reason for high performance. And that is that I've been able to hire a number of brand new teachers to the profession. Four out of my ten teachers are brand new to the profession and that has been wonderful, because I've been able to do the training. They haven't learned any bad habits and baggage. It's been very, very positive because not only do they come with all the enthusiasm of someone who's new to the profession but they're very green and very ready for training, and that's been a real positive.

Thus, in the interview process, Mikels looks for a passion for teaching and informs candidates of the school's use of direct instruction. Once hired, the new teacher is sent to a week-long direct instruction training session sponsored by the school district. Mikels said: "They come to us with a good background from that week. There's a common language and we can take it further and refine it."

While the school does have a bilingual aide who works in classrooms and helps with vocabulary building and comprehension strategies, Mikels stressed, "But our primary approach is full [English] immersion."

Sixth Street is part of the local teacher union collective bargaining agreement. Teachers are, therefore, evaluated in the same manner as teachers at other regular public schools in the district. For brand new teachers, Mikels conducts three formal classroom observations in a teacher's first year, two observations in the second year, one in the third, and then one observation every other year. New teachers also get an informal mentor teacher when they join the staff.

Mikels spends a great deal of time in the classroom, which she said makes a big difference: "The teachers know what I expect." She expects every minute of classroom time to be used well: "We believe in bell-to-bell instruction. You'll see kids working and teachers instructing by 8:05 a.m."

There is a great deal of teacher collaboration at Sixth Street. "We have a consensus model here," points out Mikels, "so any of the programs we adopt don't come as a top-down decision, they come as a result of our conversations and our consensus decison-making as an entire group. There are no resistors because this is something we decide as a team." She goes on to say: "Probably this is a significant part of our achievement: We meet together every Wednesday afternoon and we have minimum days every Friday, and meet as grade-level teams scoring student writing, scoring other student assessments, planning for interventions, designing instruction together."

Mikels and her staff spend one day a month doing vertical articulation to ensure that the educational activities in one grade fit with the activities in other grades. Those activities that are found not to fit are weeded out and those things that are added must, said Mikels, "match our philosophy so that we don't feel we are fragmented and going in different directions."

Staff development at Sixth Street has been influenced greatly by the work of educator Ruby Payne, a well-known authority on the effect of poverty on children's learning behaviors. Payne's work addresses topics such as why students with inter-generational poverty backgrounds fear being educated and the hidden rules that govern how children behave in their social classes. Payne, who operates a consulting business called aha!Process, Inc.,

> Four out of my ten teachers are brand new to the profession and that has been wonderful, because I've been able to do the training. They haven't learned any bad habits and baggage.

offers training sessions that use understanding of poverty to improve reading and math skills, meet standards and test score goals, and prevent school violence.

All staff members at Sixth Street have gone through Payne's training. Mikels said that because of the training teachers "have a full understanding of the family and the mental model that the students come from, as well as having an understanding of how these kids learn and those things that may interrupt their learning because of their background." In fact, one of the teachers at Sixth Street has become a trainer in the Payne model.

Another influence on staff development is R. J. Marzona's research on homework. Mikels explains: "He has studied homework, what's the right amount and when do you give homework. Also, he looks at what kind of homework and how important is feedback when the student turns it in." In general, Mikels said, "Our staff development is excellent. From the new teacher induction, it's a full week, and we do several breakouts during the year where we address unique areas."

Sixth Street developed its own academic standards, called "essential" or "power" standards, which are linked to the state academic content standards and the standards-aligned state tests. Mikels said, "We do long-range plans for the whole year and they're all developed around the state standards." In addition to long-range plans, she noted, "we have the

Mikels spends a great deal of time in the classroom, which she said makes a big difference: "The teachers know what I expect."

trimester and monthly benchmarks based on the essential standards, so it's the foundation for everything we do."

Explaining the benchmarking system, Mikels said, "We bring in the materials we use and the objectives that we teach, and coordinate them on a trimester basis and develop the benchmarks that go with them." Specifically, she said: "The teachers turn into me at the end of every month their benchmarks for their class, everything from running record scores to theme assessments. We're always looking at data to inform our decision-making and we're always being held accountable to make sure that that data is what we're using to drive instruction."

Mikels disagrees with those who argue that the state standards are too difficult. At Sixth Street, the emphasis on standards-based instruction has paid off. Mikels pointed out: "This last year I had 80 percent of my third graders score proficient in math on the state test and we were pushing them even into some fourth grade standards. They were doing double-digit multiplication; they were doing double-digit division. It's about expectations."

Mikels and her staff use student test scores as diagnostic instruments and as tools to inform the educational activities at the school. According to Mikels:

> We begin by taking a look [at the state test scores] and seeing where the deficiencies are with the kids. We design instruction [around the scores], deciding how we might do interventions, after-school programs, and other things to address those who have gaps. That's where we start, we do our school plan from that, all the programs that we adopt are based on something we saw in the data. We definitely live by data here. It is extremely important to us, without it it's just your best guess.

Despite the criminal activities in the area around the school, Sixth Street has few discipline and safety problems. In fact, the school has the best discipline record in the district. Part of the reason for this success is the amount of schoolwork required of students. Mikels said: "There isn't time to get into too much [trouble]. They're supervised and working hard all the time, so that's a huge piece of it right there."

Good behavior is also reinforced by the school's character education program. All students in the third through sixth grades carry a so-called "premier agenda," a booklet that contains their homework assignments and a character insert that includes 36 character qualities. Every Monday morning, students attend a 30-minute assembly focused on one or a group of the character traits. At the assembly, a teacher does a PowerPoint presentation on the trait of the week. Teachers then watch for students exhibiting the trait that week and give citizenship awards to those students.

"We design instruction [around the scores], deciding how we might do interventions, after-school programs, and other things to address those who have gaps."

Mikels and her staff have completely re-thought the issue of parental involvement. The school originally had a parent compact which required parents to serve an hour at the school once a month. However, Mikels found that this requirement amounted to little more than parents coming into the school to pour Kool-Aid. It was decided that the real goal should be parental involvement in a child's academic progress.

The K–3 teachers decided to give up two of their four monthly shortened planning days in order to meet with parents twice a month. At these meetings, teachers have homework folders for each child. If there's anything specific that the child needs to work on or if there are any particular learning gaps, that information is provided to the parents. The response has been impressive, with about 85 percent of parents meeting with teachers. Teachers in third through sixth grades send home weekly progress reports to families and call in parents as the need arises.

The school has also purchased standards-based educational games that families can play at home. Families agree to play the games for a half-hour a night and read with their child for 20 minutes. These activities constitute the major homework that every family is given.

It is often said that poor parents or parents from certain ethnic or cultural backgrounds place a low value on education. Mikels disputes this notion. Success and achievement at school matter a great deal to her parents:

> It's really important to them. They have a real pride. I don't know whether you saw it in our demographics, but very few of our parents have graduated from high school. . . . The message that we send is that this is a prep school and we are preparing them for college. That's our language here and that's the language we expect parents to have in the home — that someday [your children are] going to college.

The parents at Sixth Street push their children to succeed just like parents at more affluent schools. Mikels recalled, "One parent told her son before he tested last year that the president was going to see his scores, so he was sweating bullets." With the support of parents, children take their schoolwork seriously. She noted: "You don't see kids marking in bubbles and drawing dinosaurs on their answer sheet. There's an intensity here when they go to test."

When students perform well, they are rewarded and there are celebrations. Every child who improves his or her achievement on the state tests over the year before is given a personal organizer. Trips to Knott's Berry Farm were given to those students who moved up to the proficiency level, while trips to see a movie were given to another group that moved up one performance level, such as from "below basic" to "basic."

Every year at a school assembly, a goal is set for the state test. This year the goal was to achieve a level 10 "similar schools" ranking, which is the top rank given to schools with similar demographics. Mikels has just received word that her school achieved the goal, and she is planning a celebration for the children.

When asked what she finds most helpful among the various freedoms

> Mikels recalled, "One parent told her son before he tested last year that the president was going to see his scores, so he was sweating bullets."

given to charter schools, Mikels responds by citing financial flexibility. The funds she receives contain no strings, unlike a lot of the money that goes to regular public schools. "By getting all the money," she observes, "I'm able to make the decisions each year about what's important for us."

For example, if upgrading computers is the budget priority for the year, she can do that. All her teachers now have laptops and state-of-the-art desktop computers. With satisfaction, she said, "I'm operating right now at over $200,000 in the black and that's still purchasing everything we need."

CHAPTER THREE

BUILDING A STRUCTURE FOR SUCCESS

The teachers and the staff have taken over the job of developing instructional and educational policy. And that to me is one of the most exciting things we've done.
— DIANE PRITCHARD, PRINCIPAL

Montague Charter School, Grades K–5
Pacoima, California

THE TOWN OF PACOIMA IS LOCATED outside Los Angeles in the San Fernando Valley. Don't expect to find any pampered and bejeweled Valley girls here, however. Pacoima is a tough working-class enclave. Drive around its streets and one can feel the grittiness of the place.

One is more likely to see an auto body shop than a Starbucks. The residences have a certain tired look. Crime is part of the landscape. Yet turn up Montague Avenue and one comes upon an educational diamond in this rough town — Montague Charter School.

Diane Pritchard is the principal at Montague. A soft-spoken, mature woman with a coif of brown hair, Pritchard looks like the kindly aunt everyone wishes they had. Sitting down and chatting over a tray lunch of sandwiches and chips from the school cafeteria, it quickly becomes apparent that beneath the kindly aunt exterior is a woman of great experience and motivation.

Raised in poverty in abusive foster homes, Pritchard never thought about going to college. "I thought you had to be wealthy to go to college," she said. But after marrying, she and her husband put each other through college, both earning degrees in history and political science. After spending 10 years in

---

The Model

▸ Grade-level teams of teachers and other staff who have real decision-making authority

▸ Direct-instruction teaching methodology and curricula emphasizing practice and review

▸ Unique on-campus reading intervention clinic that teaches children how sounds are made

▸ Full English immersion for English language learners

▸ Students assessed often; teachers discuss the assessment results weekly

▸ After-school tutoring and Saturday classes

▸ Thorough analysis of test data, including using data as a check against grade inflation

▸ Teaching coaches and teachers alternate teaching days and provide feedback to each other

---

banking, she became a teacher in Los Angeles in 1966. When busing for racial integration came to the district in the 1970s, she became an integration coordinator, overseeing three schools. A camping program she created was cited as the only successful integration project in all of the Los Angeles school district.

She then went to East Los Angeles where she first encountered English language learners. She became an assistant principal at a small school in Tujunga, which had a high special-education population. This proved to be an invaluable experience for her. Then it was on to a principalship at a gifted magnet school. After this incredibly varied career, she came to Montague and has been its leader for 13 years. Pritchard believes that length of service is important:

> I think that does make a difference in reform. I think continuity in leadership is really important to a project. Whether it's the principal or the assistant principal or the group leaders, I think that's the first thing that makes things happen at a school.

Pritchard needed all her experience to deal with the myriad of challenges she faced at Montague. There were problems with student behavior. The staff felt that the community was unsafe. Few parents showed up at school meetings. Teachers felt disconnected from the curriculum, from the administration, and from each other. Decisions were made in a top-down manner; teachers stayed in their classrooms and went home at the last bell.

In response, Pritchard decided that what the school needed was a change in structure so that all voices could be heard and valued. She divided up the school into grade-level teams and gave them decision-making authority for each grade level. Further, she explains:

> Everybody has one vote. The custodians, the principal. Our governance has evolved to four policymaking councils. And the policies are ratified by the board. But every full-time employee serves on a policymaking council. And parents too, of course. But everybody has a voice. We've gone from an old-fashioned school with top-down policy where the teachers never had a chance to say that this is not working for kids, to a school where everybody has a voice and sometimes it becomes very cumbersome. . . .But, in the process, the teachers and the staff have taken over the job of developing instructional and educational policy. And that to me is one of the most exciting things we've done.

She said she loves going to the school's curriculum council and listening to teachers "wrestling with curricular issues that used to be done downtown." For example, teachers are working to implement various state curricular requirements while at the same time addressing the wide array of student needs and especially ensuring that English language learners are not isolated. Yet, although curricular issues are important, Pritchard said that when one re-makes a school, one can either focus on curriculum or structure. "For me," she said, "the way I worked, it was the structure."

It was when she and the school started to focus on curriculum, however, that the idea of becoming a charter school surfaced. Listening to educators at fellow successful Pacoima charter schools Vaughn

2003–04 Demographics	
Hispanic	96%
White	2%
American Indian	1%
English language learners	57%
Free and reduced lunch	90%

Academic Performance Index (API) Growth Comparisons

2001	2002	2003	2004
585	596	639	644	683	687	704

■ Base Score ▨ Growth Target ■ Growth

Learning Center and Fenton, Pritchard felt that "we're at the point where we really want to do the curriculum piece, we're ready to go, so let's try to go charter." Montague is a conversion charter, so the teachers at the school had to support the move to charter status, which they did nearly unanimously. The school became a charter in 1996.

When Pritchard and her staff focused on curriculum, they did so very seriously because the curriculum situation at the school had become a huge, disconnected mess. According to Pritchard:

When I first came here, they were using a variety of things. In [the Los Angeles Unified School District], you were able to have different reading programs at different levels. The primary was using one level and the upper grade was using another. There were different math programs. And in social studies, it wasn't even connected, they were just doing all kinds of things.

The school received a federal Comprehensive School Development Model grant that provided the funds necessary for the Montague staff to start exploring curricula across the country. Pritchard went with teacher teams to 20 national conferences to see what other teachers were doing. She would then sit with the teams to discuss and develop the school's curriculum. Indeed, she said, "if you hear teachers around here, the office staff, anybody, we're always talking about curriculum and what we're going to do for the kids."

When shopping for a curriculum, Pritchard did have a requirement: It had to be compatible with direct-instruction teaching methods. She noted that direct instruction is effective with her students because of the language differences. "Besides," she said, "if it's not direct instruction, why do you need a teacher?" When asked about the preference for the "progressive" notion of the "teacher as facilitator" at university schools of education, Pritchard ruefully replies, "I don't believe in that." She believes that teachers should teach:

> We've been going back and forth on the definition of teaching. As I tell my teachers, if the children don't learn, you're not teaching. Because if you teach someone how to ride a bicycle then they know how to ride a bicycle. So if you're teaching a concept, the child must learn it or you're not teaching.

The first curriculum conference she and her teachers attended was a Core Knowledge event. Core Knowledge, the brainchild of noted University of Virginia education professor E. D. Hirsch, is both a philosophy and a curriculum. It posits that knowledge is built on knowledge, i.e., that children learn new knowledge by building on what they already know. Core Knowledge, therefore, provides a clear sequential outline of content to be learned grade by grade.

Thus, study of the Renaissance period in fifth grade is built on study of the Middle Ages in the fourth grade, ancient Rome in the third grade, and ancient Greece in the second grade. This sequencing of topics ensures that children will come into a new grade with a shared core of very specific knowledge and skills. Pritchard and her teachers adopted the Core Knowledge program.

The benefits of Core Knowledge are several. For students, it provides a broad base of knowledge, motivation to learn, and the knowledge necessary for higher levels of learning. For schools, it provides an academic focus, encourages consistency in instruction, provides a coherent and sequenced grade-by-grade learning plan, and can be an effective tool for lesson planning and communication between teachers and parents. One problem that Pritchard cites, though, is that in her upper grades, Core

"I think continuity in leadership is really important to a project. Whether it's the principal or the assistant principal or the group leaders, I think that's the first thing that makes things happen at a school."

Knowledge and the state standards do not necessarily align in subjects such as history and science.

Pritchard said that the proof of Core Knowledge's impact is in the classroom. She said: "My first grade in a few weeks is doing a walk through American History. These are first graders and second language learners and you will not believe what they're doing. They're talking about Sacagawea and going across the wide Missouri and the Constitution and the Bill of Rights. This is all Core Knowledge."

Given the school's adherence to Core Knowledge, it comes as no surprise that Montague uses the philosophically similar and compatible Saxon Math curriculum. Pritchard points to Saxon as one of the keys to the school's success. The Saxon curriculum breaks down complex concepts into related smaller increments, which are easier for teachers to teach and easier for students to learn. Each increment is built on the foundation of earlier increments, which results in students gaining a deeper understanding of mathematical concepts.

The curriculum systematically distributes the instruction, practice, and assessment of these increments across a grade level, ensuring that students have the opportunity to master each increment before being introduced to the subsequent one. Pritchard said, "If anybody wants to hear about a program that will make a dramatic change in their school, I would recommend Saxon Math."

In the old math texts, Pritchard observes that chapter one would be addition, chapter two would be subtraction, and so forth. Students would then be assessed only on the new material learned in the current chapter. In the Saxon curriculum, concepts like addition and subtraction are spiraled, or reviewed, throughout the lessons so concepts become ingrained and automatic. There may be five or six concepts spiraled in a particular lesson. The constant review of learned material is manifested in continual practice of increments of knowledge. This continual practice results in students committing concepts to long-term memory and being able to achieve automaticity of basic math skills.

According to Pritchard, the Saxon lessons are highly structured and organized, so that "everybody teaches the same way." New teachers find the Saxon curriculum especially helpful because the structure and organization helps guide their teaching. Saxon requires student assessments every five days, or every fifth lesson, so teachers must stay on a pacing schedule so the student does not fall behind. This prevents the all-too-familiar effort by many teachers to try to squeeze a couple of months of material into the last two weeks of the school year.

Saxon's frequent assessments test for the acquisition and the maintenance of concepts. The assessments are also cumulative, so teachers can check on whether students are retaining skills. Individual teachers and teacher teams analyze the assessments to figure out ways not only to help students, but also to help teachers become more effective. Pritchard said, "If I have a skill that I'm not doing well at but you are, then how can you help me do it?" The assessments, therefore, are the source "for a lot of self-reflective data examination."

Pritchard said that in reading, the structured phonics-intensive Open Court curriculum is a good fit with Core Knowledge. The decision to use Open Court stemmed from the school's search for a curriculum that would build language skills for a student population with a large number of English language learners. Montague adopted Open Court before the school district did. Many of the school's teachers were not familiar with Open Court and its required teaching methodology. For this reason, the school did a lot of Open Court

Yet, although curricular issues are important, Pritchard said that when one re-makes a school, one can either focus on curriculum or structure. "For me," she said, "the way I worked, it was the structure."

She noted that direct instruction is effective with her students because of the language differences. "Besides," she said, "if it's not direct instruction, why do you need a teacher?"

training, with many teachers going through three five-day training sessions.

Like Saxon, Open Court uses the spiraling system of constant review and practice. There are frequent assessments and a pacing schedule for teachers. The curriculum has worked for Montague's English language learners, with the school's California English Language Development Test scores topping both the state and district averages.

As a supplement to Open Court, Montague has the only Lindamood-Bell reading clinic on a public school campus. Under the Lindamood-Bell program, students are taught phonemic awareness, which allows individuals to mouth the actions that produce speech sounds. This awareness gives students the ability to verify sounds within words, which allows them to become self-correcting in reading, spelling, and speech. It is common for students to gain several grade levels in decoding ability after spending a month or two in the program. Children selected for the program go for an hour every day. Upper-grade students go either before or after school so they can get additional reading time. "This is a really powerful program," said Pritchard.

Montague has a lot of so-called newcomers, children who have just recently arrived from a foreign country. These newcomers get six hours a week of additional instruction: one hour after school for three days and then English as a Second Language academy on Saturday. Pritchard said, "We really immerse them in English," and that "seems to work for them."

Critics of curricula like Core Knowledge, Saxon, and Open Court often argue that such highly structured practice-oriented programs leave little room for creativity by teachers or students. Pritchard, however, dismantles this stereotype, pointing out that she uses the visual and performing arts as integral parts of the curricula. For example, she said:

I think that visual and performing arts cannot be underestimated in the value of building language. And if I were going to open another charter school, I would do a special ed school with visual and performing arts. I think special ed children can excel through the arts. That may be the vehicle for a lot of them. Three years ago, we did Peter Pan. The three leads in an hour-and-a-half musical were special ed kids.

Montague employs a full-time art teacher and a full-time performing arts teacher. But, according to Pritchard, the whole staff gets involved in arts education. Many of the teachers extend the school day and teach art lessons in the afternoon. "They just do that voluntarily," said Pritchard, "God bless them all." She points out that 16 of the school's teachers are either visual or performing artists. "We hire with that in mind," she said.

In summary, then, Pritchard said that teachers at Montague are on the same page, with all teachers writing pacing plans for their grade level. Students are assessed often and teachers discuss the assessment results at team meetings every week. Thus, she observed:

So I think the fact that what works is first of all, we selected the correct curriculum for the children in this community. I think it's connected. Everyone understands it; everyone's been trained in it. It's monitored and there's data collection. That was the last piece we fit in. That is the most difficult. You can collect all kinds of data but what you do with it is the proof.

So when Pritchard walks the campus, she is pleased: "When I go into the first grade and I walk from classroom to classroom, they are pretty much on the same lesson. They're using the proper techniques. Everything is connected. And everyone understands."

Montague not only educates students, it also educates their parents. "I have classes going every single minute of the day for the parents of this school," said Pritchard. There is a parent intern program where 32 parents are trained to understand the school's program and its decisionmaking process.

The school runs a home literacy program that sends trainers into the homes of parents with children younger than four years old. Pritchard said the trainers "train the parents every week on literacy and what you do in the family." Montague also operates a preschool program called School Language Readiness, which the school district uses as well. In addition, Pritchard said:

> Then we have the Doing Words program, which is very, very powerful. It's based on research out of New Zealand. It's a literacy program. For the first hour of every day, the parents come in and work with their children and the teacher. They do an Open Court workshop at that time. At the end of kindergarten, our children are writing three and four independent sentences.

The participation rate among kindergarten parents in Doing Words is about 80 percent.

On the school's literacy night, which has been held for five years in September, books are given away to parents. So far 50,000 books have been distributed. As Pritchard noted, "So the children have books at home and I think that changes the parents' whole perspective. I really do believe in the parent piece."

The school has a strong relationship with the local community college, Mission College. Staff from the college provide various services, including foster care training, GED classes for parents, and citizenship courses. Most of these classes are held at Montague.

Montague also runs extended library hours, as there is no library in the area. Parents are welcome to come to the library before and after school. Pritchard said that prior to her arrival, parents were blamed for all the faults of the children. Now, instead of looking for scapegoats to blame, the school has high expectations of students and that has made a huge difference.

The school, said Pritchard, has become the center of the community: "I think the fact that parents can come to this school — we're a full-service school; we do food, we do clothing, we do emergencies, we do counseling — has made us the heart of this community and I think they've linked with it."

The school offers after-school tutoring from 2:30 to 5:30 p.m. and next year will offer before-school tutoring as well. Also, the school week does not end on Fridays. "Saturdays are just packed full," said Pritchard. This year the school is doing math enrichment on Saturdays, as well as multimedia projects for gifted children. There is also an ESL academy, plus accelerated reading, a writing lab, test-taking classes, and classes for parents.

> Many of the teachers extend the school day and teach art lessons in the afternoon. "They just do that voluntarily," said Pritchard, "God bless them all."

Testing is a very important tool at Montague. The school uses different types of tests. There are, of course, the state standardized tests, which Pritchard said "we look at very carefully." Also, she said the school has purchased an early literacy test from Renaissance Learning, "which is one of the best tests I have seen" and which is administered at the beginning, middle, and end of the year. She and her teachers spend a great deal of time analyzing this testing data.

In addition, both Saxon and Open Court have regular tests and teachers discuss the results at team meetings. The school has a color coding system for each individual child as to whether he or she is above or below the desired performance benchmark. Green is above, while red is below. This system allows teachers to visualize their classroom, so, said Pritchard, "if a teacher has a lot of reds and not very many greens, then we can talk about how to fix that." The school now uses test data to direct classroom instruction.

For Pritchard, data is key. She sits on the screening committee, which meets every Monday. The committee looks at testing and other performance data to identify which students are not achieving. Solutions are then worked out with the teacher.

Student grades must be backed up by the testing data. Pritchard spends a couple of hours examining each teacher's student report cards and compares the grades to the testing data. If there is a conflict, she will discuss it with the teacher.

"When I go into the first grade and I walk from classroom to classroom, they are pretty much on the same lesson. They're using the proper techniques. Everything is connected."

When looking for teachers at Montague, Pritchard has a checklist. She wants someone with background knowledge, organizational skills, communications skills, and a willingness to work collaboratively with other teachers. She also wants someone who is comfortable in the community and can relate to the parents. "The parent link is really important," said Pritchard. "That shows respect to the community and the children."

She also wants teachers with a good work ethic. "There's a lot of hard work to do," she said. "I'm not the only one who comes in at 4:30 a.m." Many teachers arrive very early, and by 7:30 a.m. the parking lots are closed. She points out, "We start at 7:50 a.m. and teachers stay late too."

In interviews, teachers are asked a set series of questions, including, for example, how they would manage a disruptive child. Prospective teachers are asked to do demonstration lessons. She looks for people who are self-starters, creative, flexible, and have talents in the arts. She also wants people who can bring things that enhance the school and which are not currently present at the school. Finally, she said, "I look for someone who's bright and shiny and says, 'I've always wanted to teach kids.'"

Improving the quality of Montague's teacher corps has been a long process. Pritchard said that when she first started at the school, many changes needed to be made. She said that she used to think that reform was easy, but it has taken years for things to get better. The teacher quality problem was not helped when class-size reduction was passed by the state and she then had to hire 14 new teachers in one year. She had to hire a lot of inexperienced teachers on emergency credentials. Now, however, the school has only one teacher on emergency credentials.

Montague does a number of things to improve teacher quality. The school has two teaching coaches. In-house professional development training occurs every Tuesday. The professional development is centered around a chosen focus for the year, such as differentiated instruction. Pritchard believes, however, that the best teacher quality tool at the school is the grade-level teacher team meeting.

The team meetings were inaugurated five years ago and started off as complaining sessions. Now, however, the attitude has completely changed. A teacher will point out that something is not working in his or her classroom and will ask colleagues what they are doing that is more successful. As Pritchard observes, "They're really training themselves." Last year, she said, "I had teachers going into each other's rooms and making reports back to each other." The day we visited Montague, the third-grade teachers were having a team meeting at which they were examining a joint writing assessment and analyzing writing across the grade level.

Pritchard makes the point that many teachers benefit by the structured curricula at Montague. She acknowledges that there are good creative teachers who can teach and be successful with any type of curriculum. However, she said that there is "a different strata of teachers who really need a good structure." A good, structured curriculum acts as a guide for teachers, which is especially important for newer teachers.

Pritchard believes that the best way to ensure teacher quality is to be in the classroom. She does not do formal observations, but visits classrooms weekly. She takes her curriculum guide, such as the Open Court manual for a particular grade, and compares what the teacher is doing with what he or she should be doing. She makes notes and discusses them with teachers. In addition, her two teaching coaches/instruction directors, one for Open Court and the other for math and social studies, have set up a system of reciprocal teaching in which the coaches go into classrooms for five

This year the school is doing math enrichment on Saturdays, as well as multimedia projects for gifted children. There is also an ESL academy, plus accelerated reading, a writing lab, test-taking classes, and classes for parents.

> Student grades must be backed up by the testing data. Pritchard spends a couple of hours examining each teacher's student report cards and compares the grades to the testing data.

days. The coach teaches one day and the teacher teaches the next day. The two are co-teaching, observing each other and providing valuable feedback. Pritchard said that this system is a powerful model.

Because of the structured curricula and the pacing schedules, Pritchard said: "I know where every single teacher is. I can tell you instructionally where they are and where they need to go." In other words, she noted: "Basically the grade level is on the same page. I like that and I think it makes sense for the kids."

Pritchard formally evaluates her teachers using state professional standards. She has teachers set up their goals for the year, and at the end of the year they discuss whether they have met them. She wants to see growth. Student test scores are taken into consideration.

She is open with her teachers, which encourages teachers to talk with her when they are struggling with something. She noted, "At this school, nobody minds coming in and telling me, 'I can't do this.'" In fact, she said: "I have teachers coming in all the time telling me this lesson doesn't work and how do we do this or that. There are a lot of those informal discussions."

Montague's teachers are members of the Los Angeles teachers' union. In fact, the school was the first unionized charter school in the state. Pritchard said that as a conversion charter, the teachers would never have agreed to convert without bringing the union. She said, however, that the union has not been a problem. She does not have any problems with union work rules, and if she does she said that the school asks for a waiver. Even with the union, some teachers retired or left when the school went charter and when the charter was renewed. About half the faculty is new since the time of the original charter. As Pritchard observes, the teachers who stayed "were the ones who were willing to reform."

One of the consequences of the reforms implemented at Montague has been a huge improvement in student behavior. The school seldom has student discipline problems. As Pritchard said, "My whole philosophy is that the best discipline policy is an exciting classroom."

The school seldom has student discipline problems. As Pritchard said, "My whole philosophy is that the best discipline policy is an exciting classroom."

Pritchard manages the budget and said the school is fiscally sound and has had eight years of good audits. However, she said: "I have had to learn a lot! That's a big, big job. Down the line when I retire I'm going to recommend that an accountant come in and do a lot of the fiscal database stuff because it is a big job."

Despite the "big job," Pritchard believes that flexibility over the budget is one of the best things about being a charter school. The school can spend its money on its highest priority. As Pritchard said, "If you look at our budget, most of it goes to the children." She gets less money than other district schools, but she is able to direct it where it will make the most impact.

Besides the budget flexibility, Pritchard points to the freedom to choose curricula. Montague was able to adopt Saxon Math even though the district had not approved it. She said that curricula freedom allows the school to try different things, and if they do not work they can be thrown out and replaced with something better.

For Pritchard, her time at Montague has been the most rewarding of her long career:

> It's really been a journey to be at this school. Of all the experience that I've had, this has been the most rewarding because I was sent here by a superintendent to do certain things because things weren't happening at this school. To see where we were before and where we are now, it's like night and day. Absolute night and day.

CHAPTER FOUR

A CHARACTER-CHANGING CHARTER

A lot of kids' parents were murdered in front of them. So we had a lot of behavioral problems.

— LISA BLAIR, PRINCIPAL

Ernest C. Reems Charter School, Grades K–8
Oakland, California

WALK UP TO THE GATE OF REEMS CHARTER SCHOOL and one is met not by a gaggle of smiling, shouting children, but by a big burly security guard in a black t-shirt with a large badge slung around his neck. He eyes you suspiciously, asks you to state your business, and walkie-talkies the school office before letting you in. Immediate message: This is one tough neighborhood.

Oakland has many such neighborhoods. American Indian Public Charter School is in one, Reems is in another. The school's facilities look old and worn. But looks are definitely deceiving in this case. Enter the school's office and one is met by an energetic team, captained by principal Lisa Blair.

An articulate and affable woman, Blair makes visitors feel welcome immediately. She explains that she has a non-traditional history for a principal. She started as a career counselor at Loyola Marymount University and the University of Southern California. She then ran an anti-discrimination organization in Kansas and worked for the Greater Kansas City Chamber of Commerce in a development program.

> **The Model**
>
> ▸ Compacts with parents of students with major behavioral problems
>
> ▸ Harm-reduction therapy methods to reduce student behavioral problems
>
> ▸ Practice- and review-oriented curricula
>
> ▸ Grade-level teaching teams set priority and secondary classroom standards using state academic content standards
>
> ▸ Student test scores used for diagnostic purposes and as checks on grade inflation
>
> ▸ Recruit high-quality, goal-oriented teachers

It was while working for the chamber that she became acquainted with charter schools. At the time, the state of Missouri was taking over the Kansas City school district and was looking at charter schools as an alternative for providing a better education for children. One of her friends became the principal of a charter school started by the School Futures Research Foundation, and Blair eventually became president of the charter's board.

She worked closely with a foundation that took her all over the United States to examine the best school practices. She drew on this experience to help stave off the withdrawal of the charter at the school on whose board she sat. She was so impressive, in fact, that shortly thereafter she was made the principal of Reems in 2000.

Reems was a problem charter. Indeed, School Futures had opened Reems in 1999 and the problems were so immediate and severe that the school closed by the end of the school year. The reasons for the failure were many. For one thing, there were serious personnel issues. There had been multiple principals, each of whom did not get along with the teachers. There was teacher unrest and infighting between teachers and administrators. Unrest started to spread among the parents, and there were very serious student behavior problems. Everyone, said Blair, was angry at School Futures.

The situation deteriorated so much that administrators and teachers told parents that the school would not open the next year, even before the final decision had been made. Blair said that it was a combination of bad management and bad personnel relationships. Also, she observed, "I would think that accountability was not a word that was used here very often." Although the school's previous crew claimed to be focused on student achievement, Blair said, "I didn't see too many signs of it."

One of the first things she did was to have all the students assessed. She found that none of the report cards she had seen reflected the state of student knowledge on the oral and written assessments. In other words, the grading procedure had been a farce. "The students," she said, "were just horribly prepared for the school year they were entering."

Even before she could address student academic deficiencies, however, she had to do something about widespread student behavioral problems. According to Blair, under the school's old regime, "negative behavior, on top of everything else, was something that was reinforced versus something that should have been monitored and modifications made." She had to start at ground zero just "trying to prepare the students to sit down in a class all day long so they could learn."

So, in her first week at the school she brought in the parents of children who had major behavioral problems: "I had 13 to 14

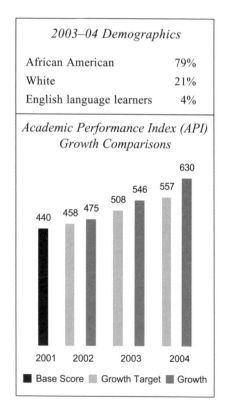

2003–04 Demographics

African American	79%
White	21%
English language learners	4%

Academic Performance Index (API) Growth Comparisons

440   458   475   508   546   557   630

2001   2002   2003   2004

■ Base Score   ■ Growth Target   ■ Growth

Blair found that none of
the report cards she had
seen reflected the state of
student knowledge on the
oral and written assessments.

parents in almost every day for about six weeks." She spent time getting to know them, allowing them to get to know her, and to feel comfortable with her. She then had them sign a management plan and compact for their children. The compact required the parents to do a number of tasks, such as spend 40 hours a year in the school, oversee homework, and ask the school for help if they themselves had trouble with their children's homework.

The parent conversations were not always easy. Blair said "almost the entire population of adults had either dropped out of school or had negative relationships and memories of school because they were poor students themselves." Yet, after some coffee and some chatting, parents realized that Blair was not trying to hurt them or their children, but rather: "We were trying to create the community they were seeking. Once they saw that, they would open up." Once she gained the trust of parents, she and the parents could focus on the behavior problems of the children:

> That's when we'd find out why we had a lot of behavior problems with our kids. A lot of our parents are drug addicts, not so much now, but then, or had just gotten out of jail, or somebody was still in jail. A lot of kids' parents were murdered in front of them. So we had a lot of behavioral problems.

To address the behavioral problems, Blair did a number of things. She hired a full-time counselor, something that most small schools in Oakland do not have. She instituted a harm-reduction program. Harm-reduction therapy is designed to monitor and manage addiction while one is moving out of it. Blair observed: "It just made sense to me that if you have a bad habit, it's the same thing as an addiction or it may become an addiction later in life. So if they were using those principles with adults then they should be able to use those same principles with kids."

Two psychotherapists from the local harm-reduction center come into the school to work with students and parents. Also, her counselor is being trained in harm-reduction therapy.

The school also has a Resiliency in Education program. Blair said that it is a four-tiered program that looks at all facets of resiliency involving parents, students, teachers, and staff. The program focuses on curriculum, character development, and building self-esteem.

The school also has a set of seven "guiding principles" for the students that are posted in every classroom. These principles address issues such as unity and faith. Blair said, "We have to teach values and accountability to the students and to the parents." Each classroom reinforces the guiding principles every morning. "I see a difference," said Blair, "when we don't start the morning out with the principles." When any student is sent to her, she always refers to the principles, asking, "What didn't happen with the guiding principles?"

The principles are now so ingrained in the children that they will use them when interacting with each other. The children are also using the behavioral guidelines at home. Blair observes: "We can see it with the younger sisters and brothers that are coming in, that live in the same household. The younger sisters and brothers are coming in with the same value structure that [the older siblings] gained here."

Blair also said that character education is very important at Reems. "So many of our kids," she noted, "while on their way to school, were coming to school and passing the police or drug addicts, or getting accosted by gangs that they really needed to sit down and talk about what happened before they went into their day." The school uses counseling and theme-oriented character development to help students overcome the negative influences in their surrounding environment.

With all these efforts, parents started to see changes in their children. Many started to come to the school asking for help. Blair tells her teachers to be in constant communication with the parents, letting them know when a child is doing poorly or when there is something good to report because "a parent needs to hear the successes just as much as he needs to hear the concerns."

Blair tells her teachers to be in constant communication with the parents, letting them know when a child is doing poorly or when there is something good to report because "a parent needs to hear the successes just as much as he needs to hear the concerns."

Using some state grant money, she pays a number of her teachers to go out to the homes of parents. Parents have reciprocated by volunteering a great many hours every year at the school. Blair said: "I think we had 10,000 hours of volunteer time. And that's pretty much our average."

Whereas before, parents were disconnected and angry at the school, they are now an integral part of the Reems community. As Blair observed with satisfaction: "We've developed a family here. It's an important factor in the academic achievement that we're making."

With the full commitment of parents and teachers, the children at Reems are responding. Blair said: "I tell my teachers that our students must learn because they are capable. Everyone is capable. All you have to do is find the flame and light it." The key is to understand that "students want to learn." "In fact," she said with surprise, "I was in the classroom yesterday evening and a student asked for more homework. I was shocked because [teachers] tell me these stories, but rarely do I hear it [firsthand]."

As discipline and behavior improved, teaching could occur because "if it's quiet in the classroom," said Blair, "you're more likely to learn." If a student acts out in class, the teacher may call a parent immediately, or the student may get after-school detention, or there may be, in a worst-case scenario, a one-day suspension.

If improving student behavior and mobilizing parents in a positive way built the foundation for the school's academic progress, what were the parts used to build the structure itself?

Blair examined the curricula and textbooks that Reems had been using. The school had been using Saxon for math and the Literary Place

Series for reading. She kept both of those and brought in textbooks published by Harcourt and Macmillan. Using some grant money, she brought in a consultant who went through the organization and did assessments of students. After speaking with parents and teachers, the consultant recommended that the school adopt Open Court. Blair did some background research on Open Court and decided "that was the one we needed to bring in." She also added an English/reading program called High Point for grades six to eight.

Using more grant money, the school opened a computer room for students. A key program is Open Book, which is a computerized program that assesses students in various topics such as phonics and reading comprehension. Students work at their own pace and whenever they reach 70 percent or above on the assessment, the program moves them to the next level. Open Book has been especially effective with English language learners, increasing their test scores dramatically. Blair noted, "We found that if you're not understanding the language and you're not reading well, then you're not going to do well in your classes." Students also learn to use computer programs such as PowerPoint and Excel.

In math, Blair points to a program called Mathmatic: "It's a rote process of learning adding, subtracting, multiplication, and division. [Students] get their names up on the board once they've gotten 100 percent. We found that their scores went up a lot after that."

Teachers have a great deal of input into the curriculum process at Reems. If a teacher has what he or she thinks is a great curriculum idea, Blair will let them try it out in their classroom. The idea will also be presented to the other teachers at staff development time and a decision is made as to where it may fit into the school's strategic plan. Blair said that the voices of teachers are heard at Reems because "when I tell everyone

"I was in the classroom yesterday evening and a student asked for more homework. I was shocked because [teachers] tell me these stories, but rarely do I hear it [firsthand]."

Teacher lesson plans, which have to be turned into Blair every week, must address certain elements of the state standards.

that this is a community school, that means it's the teachers' school as well."

Blair attributes about 40 percent of the academic improvement at Reems to the school's curriculum. She also gives credit to a reading comprehension program put in place by a former principal she hired named LaVerne Moore. This program supplemented Open Court and the other reading programs at the school.

The state's rigorous academic content standards play a major instructional role in the classroom. Teacher teams identify the top four or five standards for their grades. These become the priority standards, and the others become the secondary standards. All the teachers are, therefore, in sync because, said Blair, "everyone is teaching those same standards at a comprehensive level."

Because all the teachers know which are the priority standards, the secondary ones are also being better addressed: "What we find is that the secondary standards are beginning to be addressed more frequently because the teachers don't have to re-teach or teach for the first time when the students matriculate from one grade to the next." Previously, teachers at the school were simply teaching to the standards with which they felt comfortable rather than teaching to the standards that were truly going to move the students.

Teacher lesson plans, which have to be turned into Blair every week, must address certain elements of the state standards. The school also has a standard "road map" that teachers use to help them identify whether students are working above, below, or at grade level. Interventions are implemented depending on this evaluation and monthly progress reports using these standards-based determinations are sent home to parents.

Blair does not believe the standards are too high for children from low socioeconomic backgrounds. She has high expectations for her students and said forthrightly: "My opinion is that wherever you place the bar, that's where the student's going. So if you're using socioeconomic conditions as the determining factor, that probably means you're using them so you don't have to work. Then, the student's not going anywhere. But if you raise the bar, then the student is going to jump that hurdle, whatever that is."

She tells teachers right away that children at Reems are only disadvantaged economically. "It has nothing to do with their minds. Instead of creating a disadvantage from the start," she stated, "we're going to create a system of advantage."

Many of the teachers Blair initially hired were the children of professors or successful business people and were affluent. These teachers did not share her view that the children could achieve to high standards and that hard work was the path to greater academic success. She observed:

> They just had this liberal attitude that they were going to help all poor people, that they were going to help you get somewhere. And so they had all these preconceived notions about how to do it. And it was usually through avoidance versus good working through the process, whatever the process was.

She had to lay down the law that there would be no avoidance of those hard things that would help students succeed in school and life. Avoiding things such as testing and teaching children how to take tests has, said Blair, a pernicious result: "You look at disadvantaged areas and that's what is being produced over and over again — the bottom-rung people, the lowest of blue-collar workers."

Blair and her staff use student scores on the state tests for diagnostic purposes. They look at where a child is ranked, then determine who is on the cusp ready to go to the next level, who just made it over the cusp, etc. At the beginning of the school year a complete assessment of each child is done and an individual profile is created. If a student is ranked very high, he or she may be moved to the next level in a subject area: "so if you're in fourth grade reading and you're reading at the fifth grade level, we'll put them in the fifth grade." Also, if students are ranked low, then various interventions can be used:

> We sit down and talk [saying] these are the kids that need help. What are we doing as a school to bring these kids up? What do we see in the assessments that were done and how are we going to work with them? We examine these over and over again every year. We talk about the accountability of what we want and what our expectations are.

Student scores on the state tests and on the assessments contained in the curricula also act as a check on the grades given out by teachers. When teachers turn in report card grades to Blair, they may get a page of questions from her about why students received certain grades that seemed at variance with test scores. Blair said, "Quite often they have to rework those report cards, but I can only do that because I have the assessment and I know where the students are."

The teaching methodology is mostly direct instruction, but within that context differentiated instruction is also used. Differentiated instruction is a flexible teaching method that allows teachers to use a variety of approaches in content, process, and other areas, in response to differences in the background knowledge, readiness, interests, and learning needs of students. The goal of differentiated instruction is to meet each student where he or she is and to maximize each student's growth and success. Also, Blair said that teachers will use the Socratic method where students will be called upon to answer questions "so that they learn to discuss things."

Blair said that she also has a high-quality, hard-working teacher corps. "The teachers are magnificent," she said with pride, "I couldn't ask for more." Like Ben Chavis at American Indian Public Charter School, Blair finds many of her best teachers on Craigslist.com. She said that the candidates she finds on Craigslist are smart and are trying to improve society.

Many of the teachers Blair has hired have retired from their initial careers:

> They had always wanted to be teachers but the income wasn't what it needed to be when they were young. So I have a good number of

teachers who are in their 40s and mid-50s in second careers. They've brought their business backgrounds to the school as well. So they operate their classroom like a business, just like the way I operate the school like a business.

When Blair interviews prospective teachers, she looks for the quality of the individual. She wants to know: "What types of goals do they have for themselves? What do they want to see in society? How do they think they can help a community of this type? Have they been involved in a community of this type? What are their desires for their classroom? How do they see their classroom succeeding?"

She wants people who want to help others and have a purpose in giving that help. She said, "No matter how brilliant you are, if you can't engage a child you're going to have trouble in the classroom, particularly in our classrooms."

Blair has several criticisms of California's teacher credentialing process. She said that in university teacher credential programs "they teach how to teach, in theory." However, many of the programs do not provide strong internship programs, so she finds that "teachers who've come from other states have more experience in the classroom."

Reems is not part of the teacher union collective bargaining agreement. Blair said that she would not want to be part of the union contract "because that's what was causing part of the problem." This view, she said, is shared by her teachers: "A lot of our teachers came to us because they didn't want to be a part of a union. They wanted the freedom to help make decisions." Further, she pointed out:

And the other part of it was that they knew a lot of people who were teaching who should not have been

Avoiding things such as testing and teaching children how to take tests has, said Blair, a pernicious result: "You look at disadvantaged areas and that's what is being produced over and over again — the bottom-rung people, the lowest of blue-collar workers."

teaching. But the unions protected them. People that needed to be terminated could not be terminated. So there was a constant friction that was going on among a lot of them and that's the sort of story that they tell, the younger teacher from the district, particularly the Oakland Unified District.

Without the union, Blair has been able to make hiring and firing decisions based on the performance of teachers. "It has worked out great," she said. Also, while there is no actual pay-for-performance system at Reems, when the budget permits, bonus checks are given to teachers who are performing well.

The salaries at Reems are comparable to the district for the first few years of a teacher's career, but the district pays a higher wage in outlying years. Blair worries, naturally, that she will lose some of her teachers in a few years, although the dysfunction of the district is likely a balancing factor to the higher salaries.

There is a formal teacher evaluation process at Reems. Some of the factors taken into consideration include whether teachers work well with individual students, how well they work with differentiated learning, how well they work with other teachers, plus issues of behavior, accountability, and classroom management.

The union was not the only thing that irritated the teachers who came to Reems. Blair relates that teachers were thoroughly dissatisfied with Oakland Unified School District and its policies. For example, there were constant curriculum changes that required new training for teachers. Blair said, "There was no stability in education [policies]." Further, in the district, teachers were not supported by their principals, and they are happy to be at Reems because Blair supports her staff.

In Blair's view, heading up a charter school gives her the freedom to succeed: "The most important thing is that you can make changes when you want to. We're not bound by a bureaucracy and we're not bound by a union."

Blair also has a great deal of flexibility in dealing with budget issues. The school's board oversees her actions, but she has freedom to make most budget decisions: "If we want to purchase books, we make decisions about the books. If we want to go on field trips, we make those decisions. So everything is done right here. It's like a small business."

One of the problems in the state's public school system is that non-traditional principal candidates, like business people, have great difficulty obtaining the administrative service credential needed to become a principal. A business person could get a service credential in another state but it would not be recognized in California. In Blair's opinion, the regulations in California are too stringent, "and I don't think those regulations are supporting education here at all."

The things that Blair and Reems have done — developing a community atmosphere between parents and the school, improving and enlarging curriculum, focusing on academic performance, measuring performance through test results, implementing standards in the classroom, and providing supplemental services such as counseling — have combined to boost the achievement of the school's children. Blair noted, "Our kids have seen success, so they expect success." Also, Blair likes field trips because they expand children's worldview, which gives them a richer vocabulary and a better ability to compete with other students.

One very hopeful sign, said Blair, is the performance of students once they leave Reems: "Academically, a large number of them are retaining the success they had here." Many "test out of ninth-grade work" and are "still leaders in their schools." For those who fall on difficult times, mostly because of the environment, Reems staff will still work with them.

One big sign that things have turned around at Reems involved an incident that could have been a tragedy. A few

"I have a good number of teachers who are in their 40s and mid-50s in second careers. They've brought their business backgrounds to the school as well. So they operate their class-room like a business, just like the way I operate the school like a business."

weeks before we interviewed Lisa Blair, a chartered bus carrying children and parents from Reems crashed on its way back from a snow outing in the Sierras. Fortunately, no one was seriously injured.

Blair pointed out that whereas when she started at Reems there had been terrible relations between parents and school staff, when this accident occurred, the school community rallied. Blair said: "Everyone was here helping. By the time the last bus came back with people who were injured but released, it was 1:30 in the morning and I had a full staff here ready to receive them." Parents and staff came together to support one another. Blair observed with satisfaction: "We've developed a family here. It's an important factor in the academic achievement that we're making."

CHAPTER FIVE

TEACHER TRANSFORMATION

She was our resource specialist teacher here. I was appalled. She was old and crabby and she had no skill whatsoever, no classroom management. She had no idea how to teach anything except handwriting. She was a very strong union person and I'm sure that somewhere along the line someone realized that she was not a teacher.

— IRENE SUMIDA, DIRECTOR OF INSTRUCTION AND CURRICULUM

Fenton Avenue Elementary, Grades K–5
Pacoima, California

LOCATED IN THE SAN FERNANDO VALLEY in Los Angeles, not far from Montague Charter School in Pacoima, is Fenton Avenue Charter School. Fenton is one of California's first charter schools, having received its charter in 1994. Like its equally famous neighbor, Vaughn Next Century Learning Center, Fenton's ongoing academic success has made it a poster child for the state's charter movement. Then first lady Hillary Rodham Clinton and other luminaries have visited the school.

For politicians, the temptation at a school like Fenton is simply to point to its academic accomplishments, shake some hands, and depart after the photo-op. Yet because of its achievements, policymakers, educators, charter proponents, and the public should learn from what Fenton has done during its long march of progress.

Fenton is unusual in that rather than having one leader, it really has two. Joe Lucente is Fenton's executive director and Irene Sumida is the school's director of instruction. There is a neat division of labor, with

---

The Model

▸ Ensure high-quality teaching through rigorous teacher evaluations; failure to improve results in teacher termination

▸ Non-union status eliminates tenure and allows teachers to be assigned based on needs of students, not on seniority

▸ Grade-level teaching teams plan and test the success of standards-based lessons

▸ Full English immersion for English language learners, plus English language development labs and off-track instruction for ELL students having difficulties

▸ Extra instructional time during the school year, including Saturday classes

▸ Test results used for diagnostic purposes

▸ Good management leadership focusing on cost efficiency and fiscal responsibility

---

Lucente handling more of the business and management side of the school's operations and Sumida focusing on the academic program. Fenton's co-leadership solves the problem that numerous charter schools have; that is, a principal who is more skilled in academic matters than management or vice versa.

Joe Lucente is a welcoming man with silver hair and a broad smile. Although he is a longtime educator, his background is in business. He has a bachelor's degree in business administration and has had a wide variety of jobs, ranging from managing a liquor store in college, to working in the newspaper business, to managing motels and working as a real estate broker. "I have a fairly well-rounded experiential and educational background," he explained with a grin. There was nothing to smile about, however, when Lucente first arrived at Fenton five years before the school became a charter.

Lucente noted that if the San Fernando Valley were a separate school district, instead of being part of the Los Angeles district, it would be the seventh largest in the nation. Thus, when he said that Fenton and neighboring Vaughn were the two worst schools in the Valley, it was a severe statement.

According to Lucente, this indictment is not hyperbole: "When I came here I was the fifth principal in six years. My predecessor had that door locked with a No Admittance sign on it. I had a fifth-grade teacher who was in her first year with the district running the school. Her predecessor left after repeated death threats from the parents." No wonder, then, that he said that Fenton "was a totally dysfunctional school."

Like Lisa Blair at Reems, Lucente spent his first years at Fenton just putting out fires: "I spent a couple of years just trying to get the place safe and sane." "Everybody wanted to leave the school," he said, "so I just let everyone who wanted to leave, leave, and hired anybody who was willing to work here."

By 1993, the school had calmed down and parents were happier, but student achievement was still low and teacher morale was not much higher. At the time, Yvonne Chan, the principal at neighboring Vaughn Street Elementary School, told Lucente and other principals that she was going to "get rid of the district" and transform her school into a charter school. Also, Lucente learned that out of the approximately $4,200 per student that the Los Angeles school district received from the state, only $2,700 reached the school.

This skimming operation by the district upset Lucente and led him to investigate seriously

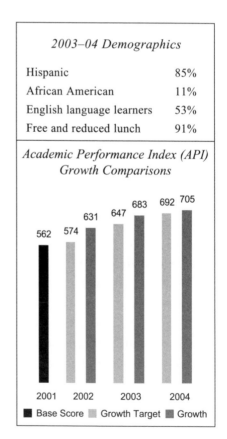

2003–04 Demographics

Hispanic	85%
African American	11%
English language learners	53%
Free and reduced lunch	91%

Academic Performance Index (API) Growth Comparisons

Chan's charter idea. After doing a lot of research and engaging in several weeks of discussion with teachers, the decision was made to make Fenton a charter school.

Lucente said that prior to the switch, people at the school felt disenfranchised. Now, everyone is involved and is a member of one of the school's various governing councils. Because of this involvement, he said, "There is no need for [union] representation because they don't need representation against themselves." When Fenton's staff severed their ties to the union, Lucente said, "it was probably the best thing that ever happened."

Without a union, "teachers here are assigned based on the needs of kids and on their expertise rather than on seniority." Without a union, Fenton eliminated teacher tenure. According to Lucente:

> Tenure does not exist. We have probationary employees and regular employees. A regular employee's contract is year to year. As long as you get a satisfactory evaluation, it will be continued for the next year. But we do not follow any of the other union kinds of rules. For example, a teacher is not automatically a regular employee after two years. They have to be recommended for that status. Some may never be recommended and that's eventually the reason why they leave.

Teachers have not missed the union. Lucente said that Fenton's benefits are better than the district's, the salaries are higher, and the opportunities are better. For example, a nationally board-certified teacher can receive an additional $10,000 in salary.

With the school's newfound freedom, Lucente went about putting together his dream school. He said, "We discovered about eight years ago that our children who are predominately disadvantaged, who don't have a great experiential background when they come to the school, seem to interact really well with technology." He has used his funds to make Fenton into "probably the most high-tech public elementary school you're going to find in the nation." He noted that there are more than 950 computers in the school, which he said makes teaching more effective and time-efficient.

The school used its money to fund extra days and hours for students. The school currently has 191 days of instruction, more than the minimum180 days, and also has Saturday classes once a month for parents and students. More days in the classroom will only help students, however, if they are receiving high-quality instruction.

When the state adopted its rigorous academic content standards in the late 1990s, Fenton named a standards consultant at every grade level to work with teachers so that standards-based instruction became consistent. "Once the state standards were put in place," said Lucente, "they became a part of our base, so to speak."

He said that those standards consultants are now lead teachers and there is a lead teacher at every grade level. These teachers apply for the position, are selected by the other teachers at a grade level, and are paid an additional $5,000. "Their job," explained Lucente, "is to make sure everyone at that grade level is performing, that the curriculum is delivered properly, and that everyone is doing everything possible." He pointed out, "We do not do a lot of preparing for the test, or test prep, because we believe that if you deliver the proper instruction, that they will be prepared."

The standards describe what knowledge students must learn. Who delivers that knowledge, however, is critical. Lucente said that teacher quality is the most important factor in student learning: "You know you could have everything else that we have going here, but if you don't have an extraordinary teacher in a majority of those classrooms, it's just not going to happen. That's the bottom line." That is why the school supports its teachers with "supplies, materials, staff development, lead teachers, with both the director of instruction and the assistant director for curriculum instruction."

In looking for good teachers, Lucente initially believed that experience equaled quality. "I don't believe

Without a union, "teachers here are assigned based on the needs of kids and on their expertise rather than on seniority." Without a union, Fenton eliminated teacher tenure.

In looking for good teachers, Lucente initially believed that experience equaled quality. "I don't believe that anymore," he admitted, "I have done a total 180."

that anymore," he admitted. "I have done a total 180." Instead, Fenton "looks for bright, positive, intelligent people who can think on their feet." In order to determine if a teacher has these qualities, Fenton interviewers insist on seeing candidates teach in a classroom.

Although most of the new teachers come from local university schools of education, Fenton also hires individuals from the private sector who want a career change. In fact, the teacher chiefly responsible for getting computers into Fenton's classrooms was a former bank vice president who joined the school's staff after deciding to change careers.

Teachers and teaching is the purview of Irene Sumida, the school's instructional and curriculum director. Stylish and attractive, with a soft voice, she is sometimes hard to hear above the din of children and hallway noise. However, Sumida has a quiet intensity that becomes apparent in her description of her work and philosophy. She said that the key component of Fenton's success is its corps of excellent teachers who are dedicated, hard-working, smart, and have great attitudes.

In the past, Sumida has worked with teachers who had a much different type of attitude. She remembers a teacher telling her, "I became a teacher because I didn't have to get to work until 9 a.m. and I wanted to go home at 3 p.m." She heard that exact sentiment from a teacher at Fenton when she first arrived at the school. Her response was forceful:

> I said, "Really? You should go into another profession." Because you're not going to be a good teacher ever if you think you're going to work from 9 to 3. Once you start in that classroom you're thinking about those children 24 hours a day. You think about them on the weekend, you think about them until the end of the school year, and then you take a little break and think about the next class that's coming. If you don't have that mindset, you really shouldn't be a teacher.

Yet most teachers at Fenton did not have that mindset back in 1994 when the school went charter. When Sumida asked teachers if they would send their children to the school without hesitation, all the teachers said no.

When she was a classroom teacher, Sumida observed first hand the incompetence of her colleagues and its effect on children:

> I feel that as a classroom teacher it was demeaning and demoralizing to know that the teacher on the left of me didn't work very hard, had no classroom environment, and treated the children very badly. The teacher on my right didn't have the skills; she didn't know what to do beyond multiplication. She was teaching fourth grade and she never taught the children to divide because I don't think she really knew how to. I got the children in the fifth grade and they would cry because they hadn't learned how to divide. She was leaving the classroom every 30 minutes to smoke. And no one ever did anything about it.

The school district had a supposed teacher "evaluation" system, but it was a farce. She observed "at a large school district the [evaluation] means nothing." She said that she and her ineffective peers got the same marks, and, to add insult to injury, "I know that I was paid less than these two teachers but we got the same [evaluation]."

Lazy evaluations not only allow bad teachers to remain on staff, but they also retard teacher improvement. Sumida said, "If you get the same evaluation every year how can you even identify best practice?" Also, if teacher pay is not tied to evaluations, then there is no incentive to improve:

> There's no way you can showcase the teacher who's experiencing extraordinary results because this other teacher who has 35 years [of experience] who has been doing the same thing since day one, top of the salary schedule, is not going to listen. I'm already getting my pay. I get here when the bell rings. I leave when the bell rings, I'm doing fine. What is the incentive to improve? Well, that's one of the things that we did, to establish that incentive to improve. . . . There's no incentive to improve if your pay is going to remain the same.

In order to ensure that they reach the level of excellence that she demands, Sumida conducts in-depth annual evaluations of teachers that lead to actual improvements in teacher performance. "If I have to evaluate someone," she said, "it has to be meaningful, otherwise why am I going through this?" In a true evaluation, she noted, "things should improve."

So how are teachers at Fenton evaluated? For new teachers, Sumida conducts formal observations twice a semester. She uses Charlotte Danielson's work on good teacher practices as her guide. Danielson posits four domains of good teaching: 1) planning and preparation, 2) classroom environment, 3) professional responsibilities, and 4) instruction. Under each domain are various components.

Armed with Danielson's guidelines, Sumida writes up the formal evaluations based on the four domains, looking at Danielson's rubrics, and discusses with teachers how they stack up. For a teacher to be satisfactory, he or she cannot rate unsatisfactory in any of the domains. She said, "You may not be proficient, and you won't be distinguished, but you have got to be at least satisfactory in planning and preparation and classroom environment because you have to know how to plan and prepare for the student, you have to have good classroom management, and you have to

---

THE FOUR DOMAINS OF GOOD TEACHING

Domain #1: Planning and Preparation

1a. **Demonstrating knowledge of content and pedagogy**
- Knowledge of content
- Knowledge of prerequisite relationships
- Knowledge of content-related pedagogy

1b. **Demonstrating knowledge of students**
- Knowledge of characteristics of age groups
- Knowledge of students' varied approaches to learning
- Knowledge of students' skills and knowledge
- Knowledge of students' interests and cultural heritage

1c. **Selecting instructional goals**
- Value
- Clarity
- Suitability for diverse students
- Balance

1d. **Demonstrating knowledge of resources**
- Resources for teaching
- Resources for students

1e. **Designing coherent instruction**
- Learning activities
- Instructional materials and resources
- Instructional groups
- Lesson and unit structure

1f. **Assessing student learning**
- Congruence with instructional goals
- Criteria and standards
- Use for planning

Domain #2: The Classroom Environment

2a. **Creating an environment of respect and rapport**
- Teacher interaction with students
- Student interaction

2b. **Establishing a culture for learning**
- Importance of content
- Student pride in work
- Expectations for learning and achievement

2c. **Managing classroom procedures**
- Management of instructional groups
- Management of transitions
- Management of materials and supplies
- Performance of non-instructional duties
- Supervision of volunteers and paraprofessionals

2d. **Managing student behavior**
- Expectations
- Monitoring of student behavior
- Response to student misbehavior

2e. Organizing physical space
- Safety and arrangement of furniture
- Accessibility to learning and uses of physical resources

Domain #3: Instruction

3a. Communicating clearly and accurately
- Directions and procedures
- Oral and written language

3b. Using questioning and discussion techniques
- Quality of questions
- Discussion techniques
- Student participation

3c. Engaging students in learning
- Representation of content
- Activities and assignments
- Groupings of students
- Instructional materials and resources
- Structure and pacing

3d. Providing feedback to students
- Quality: accurate, substantive, constructive, and specific
- Timeliness

3e. Demonstrating flexibility and responsiveness
- Lesson adjustment
- Response to students
- Persistence

Domain #4: Professional Responsibilities

4a. Reflecting on teaching
- Accuracy
- Use in future teaching

4b. Maintaining accurate records
- Student completion of assignments
- Student progress in learning
- Non-instructional records

4c. **Communicating with families**
  - Information about the instructional program
  - Information about individual students
  - Engagement of families in the instructional program
4d. **Contributing to the school and district**
  - Relationships with colleagues
  - Service to the school
  - Participation in school and district projects
4e. **Growing and developing professionally**
  - Enhancement of content knowledge and pedagogical skill
  - Service to the profession
4f. **Showing professionalism**
  - Service to students
  - Advocacy
  - Decision making

have an environment that makes that child want to walk in as soon as you open the door."

Once a teacher has been at the school for awhile, Sumida concentrates on the third domain of instruction. After the teacher has become stronger, then he or she must think about the fourth domain, professional responsibilities, "because as an educator it is your responsibility to learn and to share with colleagues."

Sumida's evaluation is usually five to six pages long. She explained: "I determine where they fall on the rubric and I write a summary of where I think their real strengths are. After I've written about the four domains, I write a summary overall about what I think they need to work on, their strengths, and what I'd like to see them doing in the future.

"My recommendation for that strong teacher," she said, "is usually for them to take on more leadership roles with the school so that they begin sharing their best practices."

When she came to Fenton in 1991, Sumida's efforts to evaluate teachers and improve the quality of teaching were needed desperately. She said that she saw a first-grade teacher conduct a math "lesson" by telling students to turn to a certain page and do the problems on that page. No instruction or teaching was offered. Sumida asked the teacher afterwards, "Did I miss something?" The teacher replied that the children know how to add. Sumida retorted, "No, they don't."

Things were not much better when it came to teaching reading. "[The teachers] didn't know how to teach phonics," she observed. Incredibly, she said: "I had one teacher who thought that when I talked about writing that we were talking about handwriting. It was incredible. I don't even want to tell you what she was doing in that room." In fact, that teacher would have her students spend lots of time in low-level craftwork, such as "taking styrofoam cups and making them into Snoopys." Even more amazing, said Sumida:

> She was our resource specialist teacher here. I was appalled.
> She was old and crabby and she had no skill whatsoever, no class-
> room management, she had no idea how to teach anything except
> handwriting. She was a very strong union person and I'm sure
> that somewhere along the line someone realized that she was not
> a teacher.

Unfortunately, this was no anomaly, Sumida said. "That was the caliber of the teaching for a lot of the teachers."

One way Sumida changed instruction at the school was to focus on the state academic standards. A standard was identified and the grade-level teachers planned a lesson together. After planning the lesson, one teacher was chosen to implement the lesson. Afterwards, the teachers would come back together and get debriefed on the success (or lack thereof) of the lesson. Teachers, therefore, got the experience of planning together and talking about what that lesson should look like. Both new and veteran teachers could share ideas and no one would be teaching in isolation.

Teachers were sent to staff development conferences to hear about what was happening around the country in regard to standards. Afterwards, said Sumida, "we talked very honestly about change, what needed to happen here."

Sumida noted that with any evaluation plan, there must be a bottom line. She can make suggestions for change, but teachers have to realize that there are consequences for failure to improve. Sumida explains that at Fenton, there is a peer assistance and review plan that is much different than the state's toothless version. Faltering teachers receive assistance from lead teachers plus Sumida herself and her assistant directors. Sumida would identify those domains where the teacher needed help. If a teacher failed to improve, he or she is fired:

> In the first year [of the peer assistance and review plan] I identify what a teacher will be doing. For one year we work on improving and at the end of the year I determine if the teacher has made progress. If the teacher has improved, I'll document that and they have another year to continue that improvement to get to the level where they should be satisfactory in all areas. In that first year, if they don't improve at all, they're terminated, no matter how many years of experience they have. If they make improvements, they have another year to grow. If after that second year they make the improvement that they need to, they continue on that cycle we established, but if they don't, they're terminated.

Fenton's peer assistance and review program contains no idle threats. In the first year of the program, she had three senior teachers facing sanctions. Two ended up leaving, while the third did improve. However, according to Sumida, even that third teacher did not enjoy being a teacher, despite the fact that she eventually earned a coveted national board certification. This teacher could do the paperwork of teaching, but could not connect with the children. She could not keep up her improvement and eventually left California for another state.

Fenton no longer has teacher tenure. Sumida said: "In L.A Unified, usually after two years of probationary status you become tenured. Well, it's not automatic [at Fenton]. I've told a number of teachers that you're going to need another year or more until you are ready to be regular status."

She will pair up teachers so that they can coach each other. Sumida will give the pairs suggestions such as recommending that they concentrate on technology. She will ask them to write down three goals: They

"I feel that as a classroom teacher it was demeaning and demoralizing to know that the teacher on the left of me didn't work very hard, had no classroom environment, and treated the children very badly. The teacher on my right didn't have the skills; she didn't know what to do beyond multiplication."

must identify a project that will improve student achievement that year and their first goal is to achieve it; the next goal is to figure out what will be learned from the project; and the third goal is how will they grow as professional educators.

Sumida said: "They write their goals together and then they start a document when they meet. I ask them to keep a reflection of what they talked about, what they learned each time. I want them to observe each other in the classroom, too. That gets them to other people's classrooms and gets them sharing." Teachers say it is the most powerful staff development they have ever had.

When adopting a curriculum, Sumida said that the school has one of its teachers pilot the program while other teachers observe. There is discussion about the program's costs and its effectiveness, and this discussion continues even after the program is adopted. The measuring stick is whether the program would be good enough for the teachers' own children.

In reading, Fenton uses the phonics-intensive Open Court. Fenton teachers like Open Court for a variety of reasons, including the fact that it is aligned to the state academic standards, unlike the previous curriculum used at the school. While the adoption of Open Court had wide support among the faculty, the same could not be said about the ending of bilingual education at the school.

Fenton had numerous bilingual teachers, many of whom had parents who were first-generation immigrants from Mexico. These teachers opposed the elimination of bilingual education for cultural reasons. However, Sumida said:

But then we talked about what the children are going to need ultimately. We want to support them in every way we can. Are we doing the best we can for the children by prolonging that time when they're going to learn English. . . .We finally decided we had to move into an English-only program, and we did.

If English language learners were not quickly transitioned to English fluency and reclassified, then when these children went on to middle school, many would still have to take ESL classes. Sumida asked, "When are they going to take those English classes and those literature classes they're going to need, so that when they get to high school they're going to be taking honors classes and Advanced Placement classes?" She answered, "They'll never get there unless they're reclassified."

Fenton's English immersion approach is working. Sumida observes, "The number of children we reclassify is much higher than any of our neighboring charter schools." Yet achieving English fluency is never easy, especially with fourth and fifth graders. If a child is still having problems with English at that late stage, then the school staff meets with parents and asks that the children not watch Spanish language television. Parents are informed that children have to stay after school for tutoring that concentrates on English vocabulary. Using private grant money, Fenton has also created an English-language-development lab for students. English language learners who are having a difficult time are sent to the lab in the morning for at least an hour during the time allotted for Open Court reading instruction.

In addition, English language learners who are having a difficult time will be brought in, with parent permission, for off-track instruction. When students on one track are on break, they might be placed in open spaces in classes that are still in session.

"In that first year, if they [the new teachers] don't improve at all, they're terminated, no matter how many years of experience they have. If they make improvements, they have another year to grow."

If a child is still having problems with English at that late stage, then the school staff meets with parents and asks that the children not watch Spanish-language television.

A fourth-grade student, for example, may be placed in a first-grade classroom all day for four weeks. The student is then ready to be placed in a second-grade class. Sumida said that Fenton has several students who have gone through this process and they are now at grade level in their English skills. Overall, she said that English language learners are acquiring English skills much faster now than under the previous bilingual education system.

Sumida is very supportive of the state's rigorous academic content standards: "I think we are so fortunate that we have something that actually states this is what the children should know and be able to do.

"When we first became a charter school," she said, "one of the things we said was that we were going to have high standards and expectations, that was in our mission statement." Thus, when California adopted its standards it was natural for Fenton to support and implement them. "We needed something," observed Sumida, "we needed to know exactly what children should learn and be able to do."

Sumida said that one of the worst forms of discrimination is to believe that middle-class children, like her own children, can achieve, but lower socioeconomic children cannot. She explained:

> If children who come from a lower socioeconomic background are not asked to achieve to the same standard, they are always going to be at that lower level. . . . If children from a school like ours, where the majority of the children qualify for the national free or reduced meal program, don't really receive an excellent education where they are held to high standards, for behavior and academics, then they will never be successful and we're sending them out to fail.

Sumida said that Fenton's students should be able to leave the school and attend even the most exclusive private schools because of their achievement. She is proud that her students are competitive. "It has to be that way," she pointed out, "otherwise what are we doing?"

The school's high expectations apply not only to academics, but behavior as well. Sumida said:

> We're doing a couple of things here. We're holding the children to high academic standards and we hope that one day that will get them a job. We're also holding them to high behavior standards because you've got to get to work every day, you've got to work hard, you have to have a good attitude. . . I don't want to just see you get the job, you've got to keep the job.

Children who have behavior or attitude problems that result in too many tardies or other negative marks are expelled. School staff spend a considerable amount of time with families, informing them what needs to happen both academically and behaviorally for children to improve. The school emphasizes a balance of good discipline and making sure children are happy. It is a difficult balance, but Sumida said that is the school's goal.

Fenton, like all good schools, uses the state test scores as diagnostic tools. "We want the teachers to see how their students do," said Sumida, "and they usually track them from year to year." Some of the teachers will set specific goals, such as having every child in the class score above the 50th percentile. She does add the qualifier, however, that events, such as a parent going to jail or having a family member killed, can affect a child's test score.

At Fenton, said Sumida with a smile, "The culture has changed." In 1993, the school had 44 teachers and all but three signed the charter petition. Today, there are 79 teachers at Fenton and only seven of the original group of teachers remain. As Sumida observed:

> Some left because it just wasn't for them. Again, the high standards and expectations weren't just words on a paper, they're things that are going to be put into place here. . . . I think that in every school excellent teachers are the key. They really are. It makes all

the difference. . . . It is that school culture of what it takes to be a learner. The parents feel it, the community feels it. As soon as the child walks in the gate, there's an attitude about them and you can identify who went to Fenton.

Parental involvement has been an important part of life at Fenton. The school maintained a family center that ran a food bank that served poor parents. Classes for parents were offered, including English as a second language, citizenship, literacy, and parenting. Parents are trained to use computers so that they can help their children, 40 percent of whom are the beneficiaries of a donation program that places computers in the home. School staff will even go to court with parents and translate proceedings, and will take them to doctor appointments. There is a referral system for just about any family need. As Lucente said, "We have become part of their lives."

Lucente has used Fenton's charter status to put his business and management acumen into high drive, especially in the area of maintenance. Instead of using the district's high-priced maintenance services, he goes out and finds local contractors who will do the jobs for much less. For example, on one construction project at the school, the district wanted $19,000 to do the job. Lucente found a contractor to do the work at cost for just $9,600. Also, when the district came in and re-floored two classrooms for an expensive $11,000, Lucente found a contractor to do 11 classrooms for the same amount of money. No wonder, when the district asked him why he did not want to use its maintenance services, Lucente responded strongly, "Because your maintenance sucks. It's terrible!"

So instead of doling out scarce funds to an inefficient district maintenance department, one of Lucente's solutions was to bring some market incentives into play:

> I guestimated that it really only cost about $48,000 to do all the maintenance for the school. And I was paying $100,000! As I mentioned, our plant manager left at the end of the five years. So I promoted our assistant plant manager to plant manager. And then I hired a parent who had certificates in electrical, heating and A/C,

roofing and a couple of other skills, as our assistant plant manager. I sat them down and said, I guestimate that $4,000 a month gets all the day-to-day maintenance taken care of. Any maintenance that you do that lowers that $4,000 – whatever we save under $4,000 – you get as a bonus on a quarterly basis. So immediately, our trouble calls diminished.

Further, after doing some feasibility studies, Lucente found that the district uses the profit it makes from running elementary school cafeterias to cross-subsidize secondary school cafeterias that lose money. Lucente, therefore, hired Marriott management services as his consultant to help run the school's cafeteria. Now instead of the two choices for lunch that the district offered, the school can offer five choices, have more cafeteria employees, build a walk-in refrigerator/freezer, plus have tens of thousands of dollars left over to help ease burdens on the general fund.

Indeed, Lucente said that the money saved on maintenance and other business-related areas is plowed back into the classrooms. When people ask him how Fenton is able to do all the things it does, he replies that "there's no magic." Instead of taking their funds and sending them to the district headquarters, "we keep the dollars here and we give the district very little." Getting "as much cluck for the buck," as he said, is a lesson for those who argue that the public must cough up more tax dollars for maintenance and construction. Lucente agreed that if all schools had the ability to do the things Fenton has done, there would be much less need for expensive bond measures.

Lucente said that leadership is critical to the success of Fenton and all other schools: "I'm mentoring officially six school principals right now. And a whole host are on the phone or email me all the time. I firmly believe that if we don't help each other, we've lost it. I have skills that took a lot of years to develop, and I do believe we need to help and share." He acknowledged "it's the teachers that make the difference," but he also pointed out that"you still have to have leadership."

CHAPTER SIX

A FULL-SERVICE SUCCESS STORY

When there's a drunk father giving me an attitude, I say, "Your kid is only in second grade, you're going to have 10 more years with me. You'd better shape up."
— YVONNE CHAN, PRINCIPAL

Vaughn Next Century Learning Center, Grades K–8
(Grades 9–12 being added)
Pacoima, California

FIFTEEN YEARS AGO, VAUGHN ELEMENTARY SCHOOL was one of the worst in the Los Angeles Unified School District. Like Fenton, it is located in high-poverty, high-crime Pacoima in the San Fernando Valley.

Today, Vaughn Next Century Learning Center is a national charter school success story with more than 2,200 students — nearly all of whom qualify for free and reduced lunches and are English learners. Student scores have surged upward. Class size has gone down, while teacher pay has gone up. Better yet, no additional taxpayer dollars were used in the process.

When energetic principal Yvonne Chan first came to Vaughn, the neighborhood was full of burned-down houses and racial tension was high. She came to the school with three security guards. Graffiti was abundant and school equipment like computers was often stolen before it even got to the classroom. Chan has been the principal at Vaughn for 15 years, with more than a dozen of those spent running the school as a charter.

> **The Model**
>
> ▸ Full-service community-based school that is preschool to twelfth grade, which ensures that the school can influence children and their parents throughout a child's entire school career
>
> ▸ Smaller schools within the larger overall school, which are overseen by their own administrator
>
> ▸ The six Rs: Rigorous standards, Results-focused, Resource deployment, Resiliency, Relationships, and Responsibilities
>
> ▸ A teacher performance pay system using student achievement factors such as literacy and transition to English fluency, plus multiple evaluators
>
> ▸ Use of a wide array of assessment tools for diagnostic and intervention purposes
>
> ▸ Twenty days of extra instruction
>
> ▸ Principal who excels at both the operational/business aspects of running school and instruction

Chan admits that she was once one of the "top guns" for the Los Angeles Unified School District. She had started with the district as a teacher but then moved on as a central office administrator for special education, Title I, and other programs. She then became an assistant principal. Vaughn was her third administrative stint. By then, Chan knew exactly "how to cross the t's and dot the i's and how to protect one's turf."

This experience with the district later helped her to run Vaughn as a charter because she knew what not to do. Chan stayed on as a charter school principal because she wanted to "stay with the same school, the same kids, the same parents, and the same community, but bring on a new role."

There's no doubt that Chan's personal ability to think outside the box, energy, drive, and leadership are the main inspirations behind the school's success. Chan said she's not afraid to take risks and that she's acculturated to high poverty. As a first-generation immigrant, Chan came to the United States when she was 17 years old. She had $100 in her pocket and not much more. She firmly believes that by using all the tools within a democratic society and if given equal access to public education, anyone can realize the American dream.

Indeed, Chan is an example of the many who have done so. She has a doctorate from UCLA after a French major and a Spanish minor, a master's degree in special education, a postdoctoral degree in computer science, as well as her teaching credentials. Chan said this is the sort of motivation that she is trying to impart to her students at Vaughn — that "it can be done, must be done, should be done, and I dare you to stand in my way."

Vaughn, which has been in existence since 1950, is a community-based school. Chan said her goal is for the school to become "a full-service, totally comprehensive, pre-K through twelfth grade neighborhood school." To Chan, this means focusing on the academic factor, the social component, the mental health of the students, development of the family, and development for the whole neighborhood.

Walk around the bustling campus at Vaughn and it is clear that Yvonne Chan's school has changed not only the lives of its students but the outlook of the community. Crack houses that were once used to be down the block from the school have been razed, with classroom facilities built in their place. Gangs have been edged out from the neighborhood

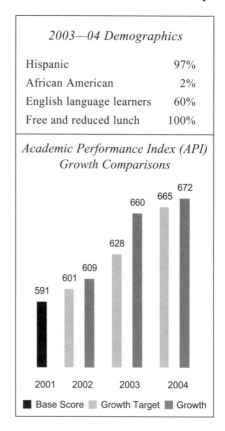

2003—04 Demographics

Hispanic	97%
African American	2%
English language learners	60%
Free and reduced lunch	100%

Academic Performance Index (API) Growth Comparisons

591 601 609 628 660 665 672

2001   2002   2003   2004

■ Base Score ▨ Growth Target ■ Growth

Chan said her goal is for the school to become "a full-service, totally comprehensive, pre-K through twelfth grade neighborhood school."

and the school has become the place parents and students go for help of every kind. Everyone who lives in this high-poverty neighborhood is welcome at the school.

The task facing Vaughn is a daunting one. One hundred percent of Vaughn's pre-K through fifth grade students are on the federal free and reduced lunch program. The school is 100 percent minority with many English language learners. There are 1,700 students in the pre-K through eighth grade program and a high school is being added to include grades 9–12. In order to close the achievement gap, the school has found creative ways to solve the urban challenges posed by its environment.

To that end, Vaughn has a wide range of programs such as a health clinic with a doctor, nurse, and an entire state-certified unit of mental health counseling. Vaughn also has programs for incarcerated youth re-entry and gang prevention. Chan summarized her community-based philosophy as: "We have it all here. There's no such thing as don't-build-in-my-backyard. We all suffer together, so why don't we all rise together? As a full-service school, we are the one who could bring together the collaborators in the community."

Chan is a problem solver. When she saw that the streets around the school were falling apart and badly in need of repair, she took action when most principals would have thought that street quality and school quality had nothing to do with each other. Waving a letter from Congressman Howard Berman's office, Chan proudly announced during our visit that the grant she had written had just been approved. Federal money to the tune of $440,000 would be flowing to Vaughn to fix the streets around the neighborhood.

Rundown streets made the neighborhood look bad and attracted gangs that ran rampant in the area. Car tires popped on the streets and students had no safe passage to school. Chan cites her initiative in this matter as an example of how Vaughn goes far and beyond just educating the students: "Our model is definitely a full-service, community-based, urban learning center."

Chan uses Title I money to give out scholarships for parents. The requirement for these scholarships includes taking classes and participating in Vaughn's governance councils, learning English, and helping out at the school. Chan believes participation from parents will cultivate a collective feeling of responsibility. Another unexpected find at the school is a clothing shop run by the parents. The clothes cost twenty-five cents and the money is used to buy crayons and games. Chan said this sort of self-help and independent initiative has helped to change the mentality of relying on handouts and welfare.

As a full-service school from pre-K through twelfth grade, Vaughn is able to keep the investments it makes in the kids from year to year. This ability is important since many improving and high-performing elementary schools are seeing a big drop in the achievement of their graduates once they reach middle and high school.

Over the years, Vaughn has developed long-term relationships with the families. Chan said: "When there's a drunk father giving me an attitude, I say, 'Your kid is only in second grade, you're going to have 10 more years with me. You'd better shape up.'"

Vaughn's enduring and now flourishing presence has made it a visible icon in the neighborhood and a mental and physical anchor for the whole community. Indeed, thanks to Yvonne Chan's tireless efforts, the whole area is now economically better off, cleaner, and safer.

Not all students have the luxury of starting and staying with Vaughn from pre-K through high school. The school runs a lottery for sixth graders and receives 190 applications for 70 spaces. This is astonishing, given the school's location in the high-poverty neighborhood of Pacoima.

Although Vaughn is a large school, it is broken down into smaller grade-level academies, each with its own administrator, its own budget, and the ability to call its own shots.

Chan said these applicants are all minority kids from poor neighborhoods, so there is no "creaming." The continuity of the student body gives Vaughn the gift of time. "Even if we get a student in the sixth grade who's only at the first-grade level, we can keep them and work with them, and there might just be a chance we can prepare them."

Although Vaughn is a large school, it is broken down into smaller grade-level academies, each with its own administrator, its own budget, and the ability to call its own shots. The school can take advantage of the economy of scale in having a large school — it received double grants from the Gates Foundation — but is still able to keep things personal and close knit. The pre-K center is a whole school unto itself. Second and third grades have an administrator. Fourth grade is a school with 160 kids. Fifth grade is also a little school. Middle school is separate from the rest.

Chan employs nine administrators to keep the quality of the staff and the level of teamwork consistent in each of these mini-schools. All the administrators have previously taught at Vaughn and have since obtained administrative credentials. Chan said they're highly paid — close to $100,000 — because they are the ones most fully connected to each grade level. They keep detailed logs on the performance of each class and have weekly one-on-one meetings with the teachers. In addition, each grade level has a lead teacher. Together they meet to deal with instructional and operational issues.

In the old days, Yvonne Chan used to walk through all the classrooms twice a week. But with so many things on her plate she no longer has the time. When she does, it's usually a fast walk through a particular grade level to see if everyone is on par. Chan said she does not get into the real details because that is the job of the grade-level administrator.

For example, fifth-grade teachers and administrators are meeting to set up a science camp for the students. Chan does not deal with the details of the science camp because she does not want to micromanage. Her job is at a higher level — to make sure that the science camp correlates with the state standards.

Seen this way, Vaughn Next Century Learning Center is a big umbrella holding a handful of smaller schools and programs. But the relationship is much closer than that of the central office to a district school. Chan said:

> We're not governing from a distance. It's structurally unique — within one school of 2,200 there are four campuses within two blocks, with an umbrella that is close by and accessible. Yet each still has the autonomy to keep the size small so that instruction is tight and the supervision is extremely close. Relationship, teamwork, and responsibility are all very close.

---

1. **Implement Rigorous Learning Standards**
   - State-adopted grade-level standards
   - Well-defined teaching practices
   - English learning and academic English
   - Visual and performing arts
   - Health and nutrition, physical education

2. **Focus on Results**
   - Statewide assessment system (mandated state tests, CELDT, High School Exit Exam)
   - Periodic criterion-referenced assessment
   - Projects and exhibition
   - Value-added research-based growth indicators

3. **Provide Resources and Tools**
   - State-adopted texts
   - Adequate and relevant resource materials
   - Technology as a learning tool
   - Library and research support
   - Meeting needs of special learners (Title I, special education, gifted and talented)
   - Structured College Education Program

4. **Build Resilience**
   - Nurturing and disciplined school environment
   - Onsite medical clinic
   - Nutrition Network
   - Counseling and advisement
   - Schools Attuned Program
   - Longer school day and a longer school year beyond state mandate
   - Structured after-school program
   - Accelerated intervention

5. **Sustain Meaningful, Long-Lasting Relationships**
   - Small campus setting
   - Small class size
   - Optimal instructional schedules
   - Sustained teacher-student relationships
   - Parents and families as resources: Family Center and Business Co-Op
   - Family connections and home visits
   - Adult mentoring

6. **Foster Commitment and Responsibilities**
   - Home-School Compact
   - Character and civic education
   - Collaborative service learning among students and sponsoring adults
   - Peer counseling and tutoring
   - Individualized post-secondary educational plan
   - Teaching as a career

The school's program is built on the six Rs: Rigorous standards, Results-focused, Resource deployment, Resiliency, Relationships, and Responsibilities.

Chan attributes Vaughn's academic success to a combination of factors: the focus on standards, team teaching, the performance-pay structure, assessment, and the school's charter flexibility.

Focus on standards. The curriculum at Vaughn weaves three rigorous types of standards into the classroom objectives:

- California state standards — knowledge, concepts, and skills that students should acquire at each grade level as defined by the California State Board of Education.

- American Diploma Projects benchmarks — include specific content and skills in English and math that graduates must have mastered by the time they leave high school if they expect to succeed in postsecondary education or in high-performance, high-growth jobs, as developed by Achieve, Inc. in partnership with The Education Trust and the Thomas B. Fordham Foundation.

- Theme standards that are developed in-house. For grades nine through twelve, the theme is international relations. In addition to the prerequisite classes of English, geometry, and biology, students also study the U.S. and China, the U.S. and the Middle East, balance of power and wealth, as well as other global issues. Chinese language classes are also mandatory so that students can receive college credit. All in all, students can earn up to a maximum of 60 college credit units.

Though the curriculum is guided by very specific rubrics for every subject area, Chan believes that teachers at Vaughn have more freedom to teach than at district schools. She allows them to select the method of teaching so long as it is within the parameters set forth in the rubrics. For instance, while the rubric mandates teachers to check for understanding, it is up to the teacher to decide how to check for understanding. And while periodic testing is mandatory in the school, individual teachers can choose how to keep track of their students' progress. Some keep detailed logs, some have Friday quizzes, and others maintain ongoing projects.

"We're open to teacher style, but we're not open in terms of the standards and the parameters of your style — the basic principles do not change."

"I have 82 teachers and the kids have different learning styles," Chan said, "so we're open to teacher style, but we're not open in terms of the standards and the parameters of your style — the basic principles do not change." Clearly stated and attainable expectations make the assessment of teachers non-subjective. Yet each teacher can find his or her own way to become a proficient educator. This flexibility within clear parameters has helped Vaughn attract those who seek the freedom to teach.

VAUGHN'S INSTRUCTIONAL MATRIX

Academies Grades	Primary Center PK, K, 1	Elementary 2–5	Middle School 6–8	High School 9–12
Opportunities	School Readiness	Academic Preparation	Adolescent Transition	College Bound
Focuses	Language dev., early literacy and numeracy intensive eng., Learning socialization	Acad. Foundation, high literacy, written communication, and academic English	Strengthen academics, content learning, smart efforts, biliteracy, college aspiration	College prep., critical thinking, research application, projects and exhibition, teaching as a career
Rigorous Standards	Preschool performance indicators, State learning standards for Kdg. and Grade 1	State learning standards for Grades 2–5	State learning standards for Grades 6–8	State learning standards for Grades 9–12, college entrance standards
Curriculum	PK – Creative Curr. K–1 Houghton Mifflin State-adopted text; supplementals	Houghton Mifflin State-adopted texts, supplementals	State-adopted texts supplementals	State-adopted texts supplementals
Results	PK–DRPP+, Gr. K, 1–UCLA Results GR. 1–STAR; CELDT for ELL	STAR and UCLA "Results" assessment, CELDT for English learners	STAR Gr. 6–UCLA Results; Gr. 7, 8–final exams	STAR, High School Exit Exam, final exams
Organization	20;1 (180-200 days) PK: 8:00 a.m.–6:00 p.m. K: 8:00 a.m.–1:20 p.m. 1st: 8:00 a.m.–2:25 p.m.	20:01 (200 days) 8:00 a.m.–2:25 p.m.	25:01 (200 days) 8:00 a.m.–2:25 p.m.	25:01 (200 days) 8:00 a.m.– 4:00 p.m. Block schedule
Learning Extension	Extensive outreach and referrals, Panda Sing, School Readiness Center, home-based learning	Technology literacy, drama and plays, cooperative projects	Adolescent health and wellness, service learning, musical instruments, oratory skills	Personalized learning plan, cohort support, information technology, economic literacy, global issues, musical band
Resources and Special Prog. (same across)	Integrated technology Library science, music and arts	Accelerated English museum study	Health and nutrition, physical education	Foreign language, Title 1 Specialized inclusion GATE
Resiliency (same across all Academies)	Safe & disciplined school environment, Nutrition Network	Schools Attuned, on site clinic, counseling and advisement	Structured after school Program, accelerated intervention	Longer school day and Longer school year (200 school days)
Relationship (same across all Academies)	Small campus, small class size, sustained relationships, Family Center, home visits	Small campus, small class size, sustained relationships, Family Center, home visits	Small campus, small class size, sustained relationships, Family Center, mentoring	Small campus, small class size, sustained relationships, Family Center, mentoring

Chan knows she is a unique administrator because she not only has an excellent grasp of the operational details, including finance and the budget, but she is also deeply involved in the instructional side. She worked closely with teachers and staff to create the school's theme standards and lesson plans. She is currently getting ready to submit these to the Asia Society for review. Chan said, "I think the uniqueness here is that I'm very much into the instructional part so that I can find the money to back it up."

Team teaching. Vaughn left the teachers' union in 1998 when the charter was renewed. Prior to converting to a charter school, teachers were allowed to pick their classes and teaching configurations based on seniority. It was not uncommon to have a teacher who was very good at teaching the fifth grade instead choose to teach kindergarten because the hours were shorter and the children were easier to manage.

Senior teachers were also able to choose the better track on the multi-track calendar. So while veteran teachers picked up the less difficult classes, brand new teachers would typically wind up with the classes no one wanted — those stacked with students whose abilities ranged widely and who had many discipline problems.

Today, the system is more equitable. The students are heterogeneously distributed among the school — everyone gets gifted students and everyone gets special education students. Chan has a large enough staff so that each team of teachers includes a teaching veteran. Veteran status is not determined by years of experience, but by a high score on the school's performance review. Veteran teachers all score a three or four on Vaughn's evaluation rubric and matrix, meaning they are distinguished or proficient in their skills and knowledge.

Teachers are required to team up with other teachers. Three teachers form a team that is responsible for 60 students. Each team consists of a teacher with 10 or more years of experience, partnered with a teacher with three to five years of experience and one emergency-credentialed, beginning teacher. This allows teachers to learn and help each other through weekly planning to reaching collective goals. The teaming also

"Kids have learning standards but teachers never have teaching standards. We wanted to change that." allows for more systematic assistance to beginning teachers and for more precision in staff development. In addition, it also facilitates Vaughn's performance-pay system by enabling the teachers to help each other without being competitive.

Performance pay. Chan and the staff at Vaughn began working on a detailed teacher evaluation matrix along with a performance pay structure in 1997, knowing that it was the year before the charter came up for renewal. A variety of reasons drove Chan to change the way teachers were evaluated and compensated. First, she felt that in order to seek out highly qualified teachers to help close the achievement gap, she wanted teacher evaluations to be aligned with students' learning standards.

Research had shown Chan that high-performing teachers produce students with high academic growth. Chan said, "Kids have learning standards but teachers never have teaching standards. We wanted to change that."

Another reason Chan wanted a performance pay system was to promote teamwork. Given collective goals, teachers are more likely to help each other improve. Chan also wanted a way to recruit good teachers. Performance pay was a way to keep good teachers who would have otherwise quickly maxed out on their pay and left the classroom to go into administrative work. So instead of topping out at $65,000, Vaughn's teachers top out at $88,000.

Chan also wanted to spend staff development money more wisely. Teachers have development levels just like kids, so staff development should be tailored to the precise needs of the teacher. With a detailed evaluation matrix, administrators can better pinpoint the strengths and weaknesses of teachers.

To help with the development of the performance pay system, Chan invited Allan Odden, director of the Teacher Compensation Project at the Consortium for Policy Research in Education at the University of

Wisconsin–Madison, to help with the research and to track Vaughn as a case study. Odden's team came each year to take surveys, conduct anonymous interviews, and guide the project through to its target.

In the first year, all new teachers and volunteers of existing teachers participated in the program. Chan herself was the first to volunteer. The following year, more people opted in. The goal was to phase in performance pay for skills and knowledge to include all teachers. By year 2000, it became a mandatory part of teaching at Vaughn.

The first goal of the performance pay system was to develop a fair and objective measure. In the early years, the evaluation matrix was limited to a few factors because the test scores were still low and the school was struggling to build infrastructure. Chan and her staff put together rubrics on five areas and measured only those areas. These included: literacy, transition, or accelerated English (87 percent or 1,200 of the students were English learners, more than many schools put together), special education (many students come to Vaughn with special education needs because of the social factors at home), lesson planning, and behavior management.

The next important question was how to measure teachers and who would do the measuring. It was decided there would be three scores: a peer reviewer score, a score from an administrator, and a self-reflection score from the teacher himself. Chan said the third component was added because she believed in the professionalism of her teachers. This review process is done twice a year and if there is a significant discrepancy among the three scores, a fourth evaluator is brought in.

The following two years math and social science were added into the evaluation matrix. In the third year, other subjects such as sciences for the middle school were also added. Eventually, the document became bulky with content and subject-specified goals. As of last year, Vaughn is shifting to Charlotte Danielson's dimensions of professional standards — a much more generic and applicable set of standards for any

> The data that come from the frequent testing help the school stay on the right track.

grade level or subject. Recall that Danielson's work serves as a guide for teacher evaluation at Fenton.

In the seven years that performance pay has been implemented at Vaughn, it has evolved from being very content and subject-specific to a much broader set of professional dimensions. It has changed from voluntary to mandatory. What started out with just teachers now includes all staff — administrators, nurses, and counselors. The standards have also gone up. So while 2.5 used to qualify a teacher for a bonus, the standard is now set half a point higher.

Despite having to leave the union and resign from the district to teach at Vaughn after 1998, Chan said she did not lose good teachers because high performers got paid more at her school than at a district school. She said:

> Highly proficient teachers who score 3.0 or higher on our matrix are making $20,000 more than before. So these teachers said, "I'll stay. I'll leave the union. I'll resign from the district. Because, gee, why don't I get $20,000 more for something I'm already doing?"

Then there are those incentives that go beyond dollars. When Vaughn was recognized as a National Blue Ribbon school, it was not just the administrators who took credit. One hundred eighty people, including the entire staff and all the teachers, went to accept the award in Washington, D.C. Chan said:

> Either all of us get acknowledged or none of us do. That is the internal culture. That whole professionalism is embedded into the culture of a total team, collective responsibility, where the collective confidence is very high. All of this adds to the professional culture.

Assessment. At Vaughn, student achievement is carefully monitored using multiple measures and ongoing assessments. These tools include:

- California Standardized Assessment Program. Vaughn is still tied to the Los Angeles school district for the Standardized Testing and

Reporting (STAR) Program as well as the California English Language Development Test (CELDT) administered yearly to English learners.

• In addition, assessment tests are administered three times a year by the RESULTS Project run by the California Professional Development Institute at UCLA. The Project includes a comprehensive, research-based battery of criterion-referenced, diagnostic tests in every skill area of language arts and English language development. These tests are aligned with state standards.

• Identification of Title I students using mandated state tests, student report cards, and writing samples.

• The above tests are supplemented by more frequent tests based on unit studies, end-of-course, or as in the elementary school level, at the end of each week.

Chan knows that not every child will meet the standards. But, she said, "That's what we use the results for — so that we can implement intervention and prevention." The data that come from the frequent testing help the school stay on the right track. For instance, Vaughn runs a huge after-school program — more than 400 children stay after school for tutoring and enrichment. Chan looks through enormous data print-outs to see if the after-school program is working for those who are getting the extra intervention. Otherwise, she said, "What's the point of having after-school pro-grams, if you're only going to track their progress during the day?"

Right now Chan is very frustrated with the district's student data management system. The district's

Vaughn was also able to add 20 extra days to run a 200-day calendar. At first the district told her that she could not mandate students to come for the extra 20 days, but Chan insisted.

system is cumbersome and limited to elementary students. Chan wanted a system that would allow her to input more of the school's day-to-day student achievement data. She has just spent a great deal of money to put in the technology for a system that can track the achievement of every one of her students, from the three-year-olds to those in middle and high schools. Vaughn is now equipped with its own computer software that tracks its students and gives Chan a better feel for how well they are hitting their targets.

Using charter flexibility. Vaughn's flexibility as a charter, as well as Yvonne Chan's willingness to push the charter laws to their limit, has allowed the school to implement the many innovative aspects of the full-service-school model. Chan said the flexibility to manage and spend money has allowed her to pour an abundance of resources into the classroom and still come out with $8 million in reserves.

Vaughn was also able to add 20 extra days to run a 200-day calendar. At first the district told her that she could not mandate students to come for the extra 20 days, but Chan insisted. Now the students at Vaughn get a bigger chunk of instructional minutes. The teachers are willing to take on the extra time for extra pay — another option made possible by the school's charter flexibility.

Chan has brought in every tool she can find to push for better facilities and higher teacher quality. She has tapped various funding sources — county, federal, Head Start, First 5. Vaughn also has a tight partnership with local universities. In each one of these partnerships, the school is the lead agent for the grant or project.

For example, with the expanded facilities that Chan has built, the school is able to house a variety of training classes. On the weekends, UCLA and California State University, Northridge hold eight different credential classes on the Vaughn campus. With 13 student

> Chan said the flexibility to manage and spend money has allowed her to pour an abundance of resources into the classroom and still come out with $8 million in reserves.

teachers doing their internships at the school, teacher recruitment is not a problem. For the school's themed international studies, Chan has no problems finding Chinese language teachers from Northridge's China Institute. She even has a visiting scholar coming from Normal University in Beijing, China's top teaching school. The universities also run administrative credentialing classes here.

All of this makes it easy for Chan to grow her own crop of teachers and administrators — guaranteeing that there is a stable supply of eager educators ready to tackle student achievement in the Vaughn tradition.

CHAPTER SEVEN

A TEAM EFFORT

We're the expert administrators but they're the expert teachers.
— DENNIS MAH, PRINCIPAL

Bowling Green Charter Elementary, Grades K–6
Sacramento, California

BOWLING GREEN CHARTER ELEMENTARY SCHOOL became California's eighteenth charter school in 1993. Its campus in South Sacramento has been around for more than 50 years. Approximately half the students speak a non-English language at home and upwards of 90 percent qualify for the federal lunch program.

The school is large, serving approximately 1,000 students, but the design and feel of the campus is cozy and personal. That is because the school is organized into six departments: the primary department, the intermediate department, the math and science academy, the multiage department, the Spanish-English developmental bilingual education department, and the physically and health impaired department. Each department has its classrooms together, clustered around its own playground area.

When the school board assigned principal Dennis Mah to Bowling Green in 1990, two other principals came up to Mah and gave him their condolences. Back then, the school was described by the superintendent as one of the most dysfunctional he had ever seen. Mah recalls that in the bad old days staff morale was low and student behavior problems were at an all-time high. Two teachers had actually gotten into fistfights in the office. There were 245 student suspensions. Mah said the teachers were too wrapped up in personnel issues to care about student achievement or the classroom.

Although not the school to which he was supposed to be assigned, Mah stayed and has now been there 15 years. He said he stayed at Bowling Green because when he got his administrative credentials, the one thing he wanted to do was to turn a school around:

> There's a certain excitement and intrinsic reward to walk in and take charge of a low-performance school. There used to be these flyers from the principals' association, things about how so-and-so walked into a school in Los Angeles or St. Louis and turned it around. I wanted to do that.

Raised in Oregon, Mah had a terrible time at school because he didn't speak English. His first job in this district in 1973 was at Bowling Green as a teacher's aide. "I've always wanted to be in charge," recalled Mah, "but what I found after I was put in charge was that I wasn't really in charge." He went on to say: "If you really want to be in charge, you've got to show other people the vision of the place where you want to go — proficiency for all kids. When they come on board and work towards that goal, then you're in charge at a different level — more like moral leadership."

When we got the tour of the school from Mah, it was obvious that he loved being a principal. In fact, Mah said that being an elementary school principal is just about the best job he can think of. However, when Mah came to Bowling Green, it was one of the three lowest-performing schools in the district. Cindy Day, a fourth, fifth, and sixth grade teacher in the multiage department, taught for two years at Bowling Green before Mah became principal. Day described the state of the school when she first began:

> I got the job because nobody else wanted it. Nobody wanted to work here. It was out of control. The behavior was atrocious. The teachers were burnt out. The administrative staff was not very supportive. There were teachers who locked the door and kids who were climbing out of the windows. It was a whole different climate. Nobody was really accountable to anybody. They just locked themselves in their rooms and did whatever. As a new teacher, there was nobody to mentor you. You were just kind of stuck. I was put in a classroom with students that nobody wanted, so I got 30 kids with various problems.

The Model

▶ Six smaller schools within the larger school, each of which operates with autonomy and with focus on the state academic content standards and student achievement

▶ A professional governance model in which teachers and administrators work together to make decisions

▶ Teachers given a great deal of autonomy and decision-making power in exchange for results

▶ Student performance data is collected in order to produce strategies to address student underachievement

▶ Teachers hired based on their compatibility with the school's vision and on their ability to manage a classroom and to work with other teachers

▶ Stable, long-term leadership in the principal's office; the principal is well known and respected in the community

---

According to Day, the school received a lot of bad press and the administrator was not very strong: "She came here late and locked herself in the office. She was almost invisible — the kids didn't know who she was." In stark contrast, on his walks around campus students readily greet Mah. Day said when Mah arrived he was very engaged: "He used to hide behind the tree and spy on us when we were walking in lines." More important, teachers were held accountable because Mah took the time to go into the classrooms. Day said, "All of a sudden teachers had to be accountable for what they were doing. They couldn't lock their doors."

Indeed, some teachers left because they did not like the new responsibilities, but most stayed. Three years later, 85 percent of the teachers would sign on to the charter that revamped the school.

As new staff came in, teachers and administrators began to get on the same page by receiving the same training and buying into the same vision. That vision, said Day, is the belief that every child can learn:

We have high expectations for every kid. It wasn't that these kids were from South Sacramento and their parents don't know how to help, so we're not going to help them. It was that every kid could learn. How can we reach every kid with different learning styles? How can we best help every kid? Every kid can learn and every kid can succeed. We started talking about colleges and universities with them — saying yes, you can go to college. These are the colleges you can go to. It can happen, it will happen. We started to help them think that.

Discipline problems have mostly vanished. Whereas the school used to have two pages of rules, today there are only five simple rules and the children all seem to know them by heart.

1. Be nice to everyone
2. Be safe
3. Be productive
4. Respect everyone's property
5. Listen and follow staff directions

Mah said the key to turning this school around was getting the people to buy into a vision and giving them the power that goes with the responsibility to perform.

Bowling Green became a charter school in 1993, three years after Mah became principal. Back then, the concept of a public charter school was still an unfamiliar one, though Mah knew that charters were exempt from most state laws governing school districts.

When Bowling Green first began to use its charter flexibilities, Mah received many grievances from both the local teachers' union and the district bureaucracy. Mah recalled that a special messenger delivered each grievance with the ominous words: "You are served."

The day after the board approved the charter, the local union president came to see Mah. He offered Mah every condition in the charter so long as the charter was withdrawn. But the teachers liked the charter and decided to keep it. "In those days," said Mah, "people didn't know what a charter was and they were afraid of it because we unilaterally rewrote the contract they spent 20 years building." He noted, "That's what the law was all about."

The district eventually made a deal with the local union — Bowling Green's teachers had to choose if they were in or out of the union. If they were in, they could stay with the district, but if they were out of the union, they were also out of the district. In the end, the teachers voted to stay in the union and the district, but to hold onto the charter status for the school.

Mah said that because the downtown district staff was trained to follow procedure, they were reluctant to allow the new charter school to do things differently. However, he was able to get much of his way because the school's 40-page charter was very clear. "As long as it's spelled out in the charter in black and white," he recalled, "we can say that the board approved this." Mah observed:

> Charters are by nature different. The district staff was now asked to be different when they're used to treating everyone uniformly. If you want to treat charters uniformly, you have to treat them differently. It's the same with students. Each kid is different, so you treat them differently to treat them the same. But the district hasn't figured that out yet.

Mah eventually asked that the school's charter be posted on the district's website, so that district staff can always refer to it when there is a dispute.

Using the charter, the school developed what Mah likes to call the professional governance model, in which professional teachers and professional administrators work together to make decisions. Bowling Green's model is extremely teacher-driven. In fact, the charter allows certificated staff to vote out administrators with a vote of no confidence. In the 11 years the school has been a charter, teachers have voted out four administrators. The administrators, in turn, have the power to evaluate teachers out of the school, especially first-year probationary teachers. If a new teacher is not performing by his or her second year, he or she is released from the school. Mah said that this way teachers and administrators learn to work together:

If I know that I can be voted out, I'm not going to go to the extreme. If they know I can evaluate teachers, they're not going to go to the extreme. But it gives teachers leverage. I don't think there's any other school in the state where teachers have that kind of real authority and leverage. That helps to build this professional model, allowing teachers to make decisions.

Teachers take part in every decision at Bowling Green, including how to spend the school's $5 million budget. Eighty percent of the budget goes to salaries and benefits. Teachers and administrators must prioritize spending on the remaining 20 percent. As an example, the school decided to trade in one of the three administrators to save costs, so that it can keep three physical education teachers. Everyone agreed that it was more important to have a good P.E. program. As a compromise, the P.E. teachers have to take responsibility covering the yard at recess and at lunch times. Mah said that this model of shared governance has worked out well.

The vision at Bowling Green is closely tied to performance. Mah said the school uses an efficacy approach: Think you can, work hard, get smarter. An important part of what makes the school successful is the collection of data and the ability to turn that data into useful strategies. Each teacher is a responsible professional who works with his or her colleagues to make decisions to improve student achievement. Mah said: "It's that professional model that drives us."

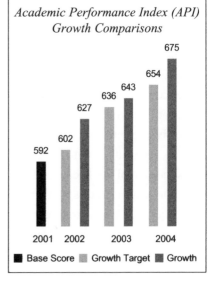

2003–04 Demographics

Hispanic	40%
Asian	24%
African American	22%
White	`12%
English language learners	51%
Free and reduced lunch	90%

Academic Performance Index (API) Growth Comparisons

2001   2002   2003   2004
■ Base Score   ■ Growth Target   ■ Growth

592   602   627   636   643   654   675

The vision is: I'm a professional, I'm part of a professional organization that makes decisions."

The school uses the state standards. When it comes to deciding what strategies to use to implement those standards, each of the six departments is given autonomy over the selection of curriculum. Some of the departments use no state-adopted curriculum at all. Others use state-adopted curriculum and modify it. The steering committee at the school allows the teachers to use curriculum that is not state-adopted, so long as the teachers can show results.

An example of curriculum flexibility can be seen in the school's bilingual department. Even though Proposition 227, a California ballot initiative, put clamps on most bilingual programs, Bowling Green did not have to follow those changes because of its charter flexibility. The bilingual department targets children who speak Spanish or who speak Spanish at home.

The program's goal is to have the students bilingual and biliterate in Spanish and English by the sixth grade. The school allowed the department to use a nonstandard, non-state-adopted curriculum because it was able to show gains in student achievement. Last year, the biggest gains at the school again came from its Spanish-speaking students in the bilingual department. About 40 percent of Bowling Green students are Spanish speaking.

The eight teachers in the bilingual department work together to identify the curriculum and modify it and, more important, they share responsibility for student achievement. However, in bilingual classes, just like in the English classes, the state standards are central and the same. In the fourth grade, all students participate in the state's STAR testing in writing. They focus in on writing for every fourth grader in every department. Mah said there is no administrative direction for them other than: "Are you focusing on the state's standards? Is every kid getting a full curriculum?"

In the multiage department, where the philosophy is that children of

Teachers take part in every decision at Bowling Green, including how to spend the school's $5 million budget.

Mah said there is no administrative direction for them other than: "Are you focusing on the state's standards? Is every kid getting a full curriculum?"

different ages can learn together as a family, the teachers have chosen to adopt different curricula and tools to reach the goal of teaching students to read. In the first grade, the multiage department uses an older version of the structured phonics-intensive Open Court reading curriculum. When the new Open Court series came out, the teachers decided to save money by adapting the old materials. That decision has worked out for the department, which has shown good student achievement results. Mah said the proof is in the results — their students are able to read and decode.

Embedded in the school charter is a school-wide social skills program, based on Susan Kovalik's brain-compatible approach. Kovalik's approach emphasizes five concepts: intelligence is a function of experience; learning is an inseparable partnership between brain and body where emotion is the gatekeeper to learning and performance and movement enhance learning; there are multiple intelligences or ways of solving problems and/or producing products; learning is a two-step process involving making meaning through pattern-seeking and developing a mental program for using what individuals understand and then wiring that into long-term memory; and personality impacts learning and performance.

Most of the staff has been trained in the brain-compatible approach. In addition, both the staff and students use the Efficacy Institute's Self-Directed Improvement System — a data-feedback strategy method.

The ability to use funding creatively and precisely has been an important tool in Bowling Green's success. Mah said that as a charter school principal, he is able to monitor where the money goes and calculate exactly how much is needed. He spends a lot of time watching how much money is spent versus how much is actually budgeted.

For example, one year the school budgeted $70,000 for utilities. At the same time, everyone was asked to turn off the lights at the end of the day and motion sensors were installed to save electricity. As a result, utility costs were only going to be around $55,000. Mah was able to project this in February, allowing the school to spend $15,000 on things it wanted but did not have money for.

Mah said the creative part is knowing how much you have to spend. By being responsible with money and closely tracking spending, Bowling Green was able to buy more of the materials that teachers wanted.

More recently, the school needed to buy nutritious snacks for students to have on the day of STAR testing. The charge for the snacks from the district was $4,000. The resource teachers at the school figured out that it would only cost $1,600 to buy everything from Smart & Final. Using Mah's credit card, the resource teachers were able to save the school $2,400. When Mah submitted the receipts for reimbursement, the district staff told him he should not have gone outside the district. Fortunately, Mah was able to point to a specific clause in the school's charter that allows Bowling Green to go with an outside vendor if it is cheaper than buying from the district.

Mah said the administrators at Bowling Green play a prodding role rather than a direct intervention one. At the end of each year, teachers are asked to develop their Stop-Start-Continue charts — what they're going to stop doing, what they're going to start doing, and what they're going to continue doing. The administrators are only involved in making sure everyone keeps to the deadlines to which they have already agreed. Mah said he wants professional teachers to come up with the interventions because they are the best qualified:

> The teachers spend 180 days in direct contact with kids, six hours a day, I don't. So who should be coming up with ideas? It should be the teachers. If they get stuck, we help find resources or guide them in the right direction. We don't want to get into a position where we're telling them, "we're the expert, you should do this or that."

The Bowling Green model is different from many top-down models. While other schools hire curriculum specialists who direct the work of the teachers, Mah said each of the teachers at Bowling Green is a professional

---

Mah said the philosophy is "to have a target you want to teach to, ask what data you need, turn it into feedback (useful information), form strategies, and teach it to see if there's change."

---

and an expert. Many of the teachers here have a master's degree; 15 more are slated to get a master's degree in the next three to four years. Mah believes that his teachers have the knowledge. He tells them, "We hired you for your brains, we want you to use them."

Mah said this is different from models in which the administrator dictates everything from the curriculum to the pacing schedule. He believes that the problem with such an administrator-driven model is that not every teacher and every student can get on the schedule. Also, there is little consequence for those who don't follow. Mah said his model not only makes teachers responsible but allows them to take pride in their work. "As professionals," Mah said, "There's pride from a teacher in their work, pride in their students."

Teachers at Bowling Green put in extra effort. The school runs summer and intersession classes for its orthopedically impaired students. After school, teachers volunteer their time to tutor the kids they've identified as needing more help. The bilingual department offers training sessions on computer technology for parents. One teacher goes so far as to bring computers to the student's home, setting them up, and teaching the parent how to use them.

During winter break, another teacher works with the parents of students who cannot read by teaching the parents how to teach their child. For many of the bilingual department's parents, a number of whom are undocumented immigrants, the school has helped them understand the importance of education for their children and that learning can be a ticket out of the poverty cycle.

The teachers' efforts have not gone unnoticed by parents and the community. So far this year, the bilingual department has already raised $5,000 through its parent group; the multiage department has raised $10,000. Mah tells the story of a Bowling Green teacher who was recently recognized by Wal-Mart as the teacher of the year.

The teacher was nominated by the parent of one of her students. The student was struggling in the class and the teacher had spent extra time working with the student. The parent saw that. One day at Wal-Mart, the parent filled out a form that said my kid's teacher did this and that, and I'm so proud.

This is an African American kid who's on free and reduced lunch — all the makings of a kid who shouldn't make it if you look at the correlation between economic status and student achievement. But we know that correlation isn't causation. And this teacher proved it. Because she took pride that every one of her kids was going to read and do well.

Mah said this is the reason for the school's continuous growth: teachers taking charge. Just as a physician should be allowed to select procedures in the operation room, teachers should be allowed to select teaching methods in the classroom. Mah said he does not want to be in the position of telling teachers how to teach if he is to support them as expert practitioners in their field. "We're the expert administrators but they're the expert teachers."

In California, all administrators are required to be teachers for at least five years. But Mah said he is now a better administrator than teacher. "I'm too long out of the classroom; I look at teachers here and they're doing things I never did. And they're doing so much better than I ever did." Mah said he has heard teachers attacking principals by saying, "Well, you never taught or you only taught so many years." His response: "That's why we hired you to do the teaching."

Data collection is at the center of Bowling Green's assessment system. Mah repeatedly stresses the importance of collecting data that can produce specific information on why particular students aren't achieving. Mah said that he and the staff spent much of last year working on assessment and learning to create a useful data stream for measuring student achievement. Because this is a confusing concept, Mah brought in Jeff Howard from the Efficacy Institute in Boston to train his staff in identifying and collecting data, as well as to explain how to convert data into useful information.

Mah said that the feedback loop on the state tests takes too long. "You take the tests in May, you don't find out until August. You have a

> In order to have a complete picture of a student's growth, different types of assessments must be used. Assessments should focus on a student's growth toward a proficiency standard rather than comparing a student's performance against other students.

different set of kids by then so it's very difficult to use the data." Bowling Green has implemented its own testing and assessment system in order to get a better sense of student achievement.

These tests include the types of questions in competency areas found on the state exam and are based on the state standards. Each department is asked to identify what they want to teach and to collect data on it. Mah said the philosophy is "to have a target you want to teach to, ask what data you need, turn it into feedback (useful information), form strategies, and teach it to see if there's change."

With every assessment there is a target. The school's charter lists the benchmarks — the knowledge and skills that students will develop through mastering five outcome areas. In the process of reaching these five outcomes, students will also demonstrate mastery of state standards.

Literacy outcome: Students read for a) pleasure, b) understanding, and c) information. Students write and speak with conviction, structure, and detail. They learn and use editorial skills that help them to communicate with simplicity and clarity. Students use technology and a variety of other tools to access and disseminate information.

Math/science outcome: Students a) discuss mathematical and scientific relationships, b) reason logically, c) think critically, and d) use mathematical and scientific skills and concepts. They effectively use the tools of mathematicians and scientists (e.g., scales and computers) in projects that demonstrate their knowledge.

Social skills/social studies: Students know and practice LIFESKILLS. They identify and articulate their application in the diverse cultures and communities of the present, as well as in the civilizations and societies of the past.

Physical and health-related fitness: Students are physically educated. They achieve, maintain, and understand the benefits of a health-enhancing level of physical fitness.

Visual and performing arts: Students demonstrate their developing talents in the visual and performing arts. They understand that the arts are a form of communication among people from different cultures.

The Bowling Green charter has four underlying assumptions for assessment:

1. In order to have a complete picture of a student's growth, different types of assessments must be used. Assessments should focus on a student's growth toward a proficiency standard rather than comparing a student's performance against other students.

2. There should be a close relationship between a desired student outcome and the means used to assess it.

3. Assessing what students do with knowledge is as important as assessing what knowledge they have.

4. Assessment should promote and support reflection and self-evaluation on the part of students, staff, and parents.

Based on these assumptions and target outcomes, the school has developed Outcome Matrices (OMs), which include the state standards, and Outcome Assessment Rubrics (OARs), which are the tools for measurement. Each Outcome Matrix consists of a set of observable skills that students are expected to perform along the way to meeting the five charter outcomes. These skills are benchmarks that show where the student is in relation to the outcomes.

These matrices are intended to drive instruction. An Outcome Assessment Rubric, on the other hand, consists of a set of assessment instruments. All instruments used in an OAR produce measurable data from which one can gauge student progress toward meeting the charter outcomes.

Mah said he sees a difference in results by teacher experience and ability and when teachers work together. In the bilingual department, the teachers have a lot of teaching experience. Of the seven classroom teachers, three have been at the school 11 years or more, two have five years of teaching experience, and one is a second-year teacher. Mah believes in trusting the teachers and giving them as much support and training as possible:

> A hundred and fifty years ago when public schools were getting under way, if you had a high school degree you could be a teacher. The best teacher became the principal teacher. Fast forward to today, we have teachers who know more than principals; you have teachers who know more than central office people. Who should be making the important decisions? It's the people who know the most and are closest to the kids. You train them by showing them the right attitude, the right vision, and then you say: Go. Give them feedback as they're getting there.

Bowling Green teachers are hired by a committee made up of an administrator, at least two teachers, and a parent. The committee tries to find candidates whose philosophy is the same as the Bowling Green vision. Mah said that teachers are sometimes reluctant to apply to a charter school:

> They're scared to come here. We've been the only charter school in this district for 10 years. People heard stories about how they have to do more work here. I tell people you're going to have to do more work no matter where you are if you're interested in what you do. So why not work hard where other people also work hard?

When new teachers come in, the school spends a lot of time and energy training them in the Bowling Green way. The better teachers train the new teachers. There is a lot of support for new teachers, including a school counselor, school social worker, school nurse, and the principal. If a teacher fails to practice good teaching during the probationary period, the school is not hesitant to release him. During the first year, if a teacher is doing borderline work, the principal will tell the teacher what she needs to work on. If by the second year there is no improvement, that teacher is released.

Many of Bowling Green's teachers come from nearby California State University, Sacramento. Others are making a career change into teaching. Mah said he finds these particular teachers focused and serious about teaching and learning:

> It's tough being a rookie teacher; it's tough on an administrator having a rookie teacher. But the teachers who are making a career change, they've got the right attitude. They've got life experiences; they're not 22 years old, they're typically 30 years old. They fit in very well.

Mah said that during the hiring process, he spends a lot of time checking references. "When you meet a teacher it's for half an hour, you see how they carry themselves," Mah said, "But it doesn't always tell you a lot." Mah said he doesn't expect new teachers to know everything about curriculum, but he does expect a new teacher to be confident. What he is looking for is the ability to manage a classroom and to work with other teachers: "If you can't manage the classroom then the whole year is wasted. Also, can you work with other people? We don't want teachers working in isolation. If you can't work collaboratively then it's going to be very difficult for that teacher and everyone else."

Within the departments there is a mentorship structure that teams new hires with experienced teachers. Mah said these mentor relationships allow teachers not only to work together and plan together, but to become friends, too. "People who like each other work together, become friends, and help each other." As students pass from grade to grade, if their teachers cannot coordinate and articulate the curriculum year after year, the students will not benefit from a good program.

Using one-time money from the state during the dot-com boom era, Mah gave out pay bonuses to all teachers — about $1,000 each — if the whole school improved. He was able to do so because of the flexibility charter schools have in spending. Mah would like to see more step incentives put into the pay structure. He said, "If your department can show increases, depending on the size of the increase, let's make it worthwhile, let's make it $10,000 per teacher."

Mah knows that the Bowling Green model, with its focus on professional teachers, is different, but he believes that it is the driving force behind the school's continued improvement and the reason why teachers have taken on more and more responsibility. He believes it is a model that can be replicated by others and one that is appropriate for the twenty-first century. The part of the model that will be difficult to replicate, said Mah, is the need for teachers to work together. Mah said in most other schools he's seen, people do not seem to want to work together or only work together on easy things.

Mah plans to talk to the local teachers' union about creating additional charter schools at sites that the state has identified as program improvement schools. He believes the appropriate model in these schools is one that puts well-educated, well-focused teachers with good attitudes in charge. Mah believes that part of the problem at underachieving schools is that principals are reduced to low-level managers instead of leaders. Mah said:

> You go to leadership or administration classes and you hear about moral leadership all the time. But what screws it up is this model we have in most school districts — very top down. The board hires superintendents. Superintendents in very large districts like this typically last about four years. Since I've been here we've had about eight superintendents. They all have their plan to implement and their plan to make them look good. They hire associate superintendents, who hire principals to do what they say. So what I've noticed in my 15 years here is that the quality of principals has gone down. You have fewer people willing to take risks, to speak out, and to take ownership for what they do.

Mah said he's looked at schools in his district that have changed principals. What he's found is that in middle-class neighborhoods, the principal does not make a big difference. The schools continue to perform well. Where he saw swings is in low-performing, high-poverty areas. There, Mah said, a good principal can turn a school around and make a difference.

New principals have asked Mah about how to run a good school. He tells them: Provide stability, stay put, do not move around, and get known in the neighborhood. "A lot of these new principals want to go downtown, do other things, and not stay in one place," said Mah, "but if you stay in one place long enough and you don't like the way things are done, you can change them. Parents," he added, "are very appreciative of the changes."

Mah practices what he preaches. While shopping at Safeway, a checker recognized Mah as the principal. Her sons Max and A. J. attended Bowling Green nearly 10 years go. She gave Mah a big hug in the middle of the grocery store and announced to everyone, "That was my children's principal. He's the best principal!"

Mah said it's great to see the impact he has had on the school and the community. He said: "For teachers and principals, if you stay at a school you can develop a relationship and a following. People get to know you. That's part of our model too."

CHAPTER EIGHT

THE BAD AND THE UGLY

CHARACTERISTICS OF BAD CHARTER SCHOOLS

The lousy schools have one thing in common: They're liberal.

— BEN CHAVIS

WHILE IT IS IMPORTANT TO UNDERSTAND why some charter schools do so well, it is equally necessary to understand why others are terribly ineffective. Although created under the same law as the good charters, low-performing charters either fail to take advantage of the flexibilities available to them or put them to poor use. Thus, charter school operators or those contemplating starting a charter school would be well advised to avoid the common characteristics that plague bad charters.

What is a bad charter school like? There are several ways to answer this question. Each successful principal interviewed was asked what he or she believed was the reason behind the poor performance at some charter schools. Given the success of their schools, plus their involvement in the charter movement, they have a unique vantage point. Also, the Pacific Research Institute sent surveys to principals at charter schools that failed to meet their test-score growth target two years out of the three-year period used in this book.

Observations from Ben Chavis

- Liberal-oriented, often emphasizing cultural heritage issues rather than strong academics
- Failure to use charter freedoms and flexibilities to break the status quo public school mold

Ben Chavis of American Indian Public Charter School has strong views not only on what works, but what does not. Having come into a charter school that was on the verge of closure, as American Indian was, Chavis is very familiar with bad charter models.

Chavis believes that charter schools that perform poorly do not place student achievement as the number-one priority. He blames the prior poor performance at American Indian on liberal education policies that de-emphasized academics in favor of cultural heritage issues and other current fashions:

> The lousy schools have one thing in common: They're liberal. [American Indian's organizers] were going to beat the drum and teach Indian language and Indian culture and all that bull****. They had smoke breaks, they had felons working for them. So in 2000, this school's charter was going to be revoked. They didn't believe in testing. They didn't know how to test. It was a mess. You couldn't have chosen such a group of idiots . . . . Let's change that term progressive. These liberals, they call themselves progressive, I've never seen a progressive idea come from them yet. I'm progressive. I go against what everybody else says. I'm the progressive, they're liberals.

Chavis noted that without a strong academic curriculum the school's original governance board created an even less rigorous learning environment than the regular public schools that the students had left. The poor academic performance of students caused parents at American Indian to protest. As Chavis observed: "All this equity and all that nonsense, that's not what parents want. They don't want black studies, they don't want Indian studies. They want reading, writing, and math. They want their kids to have the opportunity to go to college."

Chavis also believes that the problem with low-performing charters is that there is little to distinguish them from the regular public schools. In other words, they do not use their charter freedoms to break the status quo public school mold. Chavis then declared, "We're not like that." He also observed: "Usually the bad charter schools are run by liberals. They want self-esteem and they don't want books."

Observations from Linda Mikels

- Focus on unrealistic and/or unproven philosophy of teaching or learning

- Failure to understand that the goal is to increase the achievement of students

Linda Mikels also has strong views on why some charter schools do poorly. She is concerned that some charters are started by people who are too focused on doing something unique. Or they latch onto some philosophy of teaching or learning that has not been proven, especially for the types of students at the particular school.

Mikels said that these people "get so committed to the program and don't watch the data to see that the program isn't effective for that population. I'll find myself sitting at a roundtable," she reported, "and almost cringing inside because you hear when someone has fallen in love with an idea and it sounds very pie in the sky, yet the reality is whether that's what is best for kids." Mikels has no time for the fantasies of adults when the future of children is at stake:

> In the state of California, as we moved to a standards-based system of education, you ran into a lot of teachers in the average public school who were saying that "I love teaching the teddy bear unit" and "I love teaching the dinosaur unit" or "teaching isn't fun anymore" and things like that. Well, we get our excitement here and we get our fun here from watching kids achieve. You'll walk into our classrooms and you won't see shamrocks and leprechauns around the room on [St. Patrick's Day], but that's not what excites us — it's seeing kids achieve.

Observations from Lisa Blair

- Bias against testing low-income minority students; bias against pushing these students to perform up to the level of the state's rigorous academic content standards

- Often founded by teachers who have no business experience and, therefore, end up mismanaging the school

Recall that Reems charter school started as a problem charter. According to Lisa Blair, the school had multiple principals, principals fighting with teachers, bad management, and serious student behavior problems. There was little sign of any accountability. Grades were inflated and had little correlation to student test scores.

Given the situation she inherited at Reems, it is no surprise that in discussing the problems at other charter schools, Lisa Blair focuses on the importance of testing students and using test results to help students improve. She said: "My belief is that all through life you're tested. You're tested when you get a job; you're tested to get a promotion; you're tested to get into college."

This view of reality was not shared by most of the charter schools in the area, which did very little testing. These schools, according to her, had a bias that she did not share:

> They weren't taking any tests because they were anti-test and anti-standards. And I was the different duck in the group because I was saying, "No, our kids are taking all of these things." And we're mastering them.

Blair has some interesting and provocative opinions as to why her charter-school colleagues were opposed to testing and standards. She said that a lot of the people who came into the charter movement were upper-class whites who were running the schools and they felt that testing and standards were skewed to favor upper-class whites. Therefore, they wanted to exclude testing and standards from their low-income, high-minority charter schools. Blair, however, said that it is wrong to exclude something simply because a person has some dissatisfaction with the system. It is important to operate within the confines one is given: "You can't work from the outside in; you have to work from the inside out."

With her business background, Blair has the knowledge and experience needed to use her charter's fiscal freedom in wise ways. Poorly performing charter schools, many of which she said are anti-testing and anti-standards, are also often started by teachers who have no business experience. Many went straight into teaching from college "so they have a fishbowl vision." Blair said that these teachers "know they want their kids to do better but they don't know how to make all of those other things work."

"What I find," she observed, "is that a lot of people who come into the charter movement come in with a passion to teach but don't make that transition to administration." She said it would be helpful for these teacher/charter leaders to have a business background and greater knowledge about careers and career options for students.

Observations from Irene Sumida

- Founded by inexperienced individuals who do not know how to run a school properly and who have a flawed vision of change

- Failure to create a connection between the school's ideals and student performance, resulting in a school culture that views student achievement as unimportant

When asked about her impressions and observations of low-performing charter schools, Irene Sumida listed a number of problems. She said that she has seen start-up charters where "there are a number of people with very little experience as educators. Although there are those who say that this brings a fresh eye to the school experience, in some ways there's so much that goes into running a school properly that inexperience gets you into trouble."

Some experience is important. Relatively inexperienced teachers who start charters may want to effect change, but they "don't know why things should be changed or they may want to change things for the wrong reason."

> People do not realize that there is a gap between their ideals and the lack of student achievement until they are faced with non-renewal of the charter; then it is too late. Worse, these charter schools have created a culture where student achievement is not viewed as important.

Also, Sumida said that charter operators need to be realistic. She uses the example of a charter school that is going to teach students only in Spanish and not introduce English until the upper grades. Yet the state tests start in the second grade, so how is the school going to show progress and measurable results? By the time children get to the upper grades, the school's five-year period before the charter has to be renewed has elapsed and no progress has been made. Unfortunately, the "great things" that are in the minds of the charter founders may not always result in demonstrable student progress.

People do not realize that there is a gap between their ideals and the lack of student achievement until they are faced with non-renewal of the charter; then it is too late. Worse, these charter schools have created a culture where student achievement is not viewed as important. Sumida said that "working hard and children striving to do well, teachers striving to do well, and the whole school community striving to do well have to become part of the culture of the school."

Sadly, even when charter schools are doing poorly, some school districts will wink at low performance. Sumida recalls her experience reviewing the charter of an independent-study school. The school had no measurable goals in the charter, but the local school district approved the charter because the school had 1,400 students and the district had only 60. In other words, it was worth money to the district to have the charter school, despite the fact that the school's performance level was rock-bottom. Despite low test scores, Sumida said, "They don't see it as critical because their school district keeps supporting them; they just got renewed."

Observations from Howard Lappin

- The principal or the board of directors do not have a vision of what it means to be a charter school, or the ability to implement their vision
- There is a lack of either business or education expertise

Howard Lappin is the new principal of College Ready Academy charter school. He and his school are profiled in a later section of this book. Lappin is a much-decorated principal, having been named, among other things, California's principal of the year. He also taught a class on charter school development at the University of Southern California.

Lappin said, "Charter schools fail because either the principal or the board of directors doesn't have a vision as to what this means or the ability to pull this off." If the problem is that they do not have the ability to "pull it off," it is because they "also don't have one of the two expertises, either business or education." He noted that failed charter school leaders usually have one and not the other. He said: "Generally, what happens is that an educator has no business sense. That's more typical than a business-man who has no education sense."

Lappin said he is particularly familiar with one bad charter school where there is a complete lack of a workable education program. Further, there is no knowledge of how to supervise staff to make sure there is an education program going on.

Because he has seen the effect of failed charter schools on children, Lappin is a strong supporter of closing down poorly performing charters. He believes that closing a bad charter school is a sign of the success of the charter system. In fact, he said, "A few more people failing and a few more people getting kicked out would be a good thing."

"Generally, what happens is that an educator has no business sense. That's more typical than a businessman who has no education sense."

CHAPTER NINE

DEEP THROAT TELLS ALL

They held kids out in the testing. They didn't test every kid. They did not test the special kids. They held out a huge subgroup of [English language learner] kids.

— JORGE LOPEZ, PRINCIPAL

The Case of Oakland Charter Academy, Grades 6–8
Oakland, California

ALTHOUGH STATISTICAL DATA ON STUDENT ACHIEVEMENT is important when analyzing school performance, there is always the caveat that statistics can sometimes be deceiving. So it is with Oakland Charter Academy (OCA). On paper, the school, which is the oldest charter school in Oakland, looks like a highly improving charter school. The reality, however, is much more complex. It's a lesson for researchers that it pays to probe and investigate even those schools that seem like success stories.

Started in 1994, OCA sits on a busy street lined with small retail businesses. One could easily drive past the school thinking it was a time-worn office building. Inside the school one meets Jorge Lopez, the new principal at OCA. The son of Mexican immigrants, whose first teaching job was in a program for dropout migrant youths, the mustachioed Lopez is a big man with a matching personality. Warm and affable, he is happy to tell OCA's story. It is a story, however, that serves as a warning to other charter school operators.

> ## The Bad Model
>
> ▶ Mask school deficiencies through initial high performance of feeder school students
>
> ▶ Hold out English language learner students, special-education students, and other perceived low-performing students from taking the state standardized tests
>
> ▶ Unstable leadership. For example, four principals in one year
>
> ▶ Heated disputes between the governing board, parents, and principals resulting in principal being locked out of school
>
> ▶ Governing board micromanagement of school affairs that left the principal with little authority
>
> ▶ Priority given to cultural heritage on academic issues rather than core subject matter and academic achievement. Preference for ideology over empirical evidence of what works
>
> ▶ No textbooks provided to students
>
> ▶ Waste of instructional minutes due to non-academic activities and shortened days
>
> ▶ Spanish language classes for children already fluent in Spanish
>
> ▶ Bias against testing and measuring students' academic performance
>
> ▶ Teachers who were not committed to student academic learning
>
> ▶ Fiscal mismanagement, including parents paying to get their children into the school

Like Watergate's Deep Throat, Lopez rips away the veneer of seeming success at his own school. As a middle school, the secret of OCA's test score gains over the past few years has had little to do with anything being done at the school. Rather, Lopez points to the regular public elementary school down the street, International Community School, OCA's feeder school. Children coming into OCA from the International

Community School were scoring high on the state tests and helped inflate the scores at OCA, at least in the first grade or two at the middle school.

2003–04 Demographics	
Hispanic	98%
English language learners	52%

However, Lopez noted that if one looked at the scores of the International Community School students at the end of their time at OCA, it was clear their scores had tumbled: "They came high, but by the time they finished, they finished pretty low." Indeed, according to Lopez:

> I have some eighth graders here who came in near the advanced level in, let's say, Language Arts. But by the time they are leaving, they're at basic Language Arts. So they dropped. They scored relatively well, but to me it's a crime.

Also, Lopez said that while OCA's scores on the state tests appear relatively high, the school has never met the federal No Child Left Behind Act's requirement for adequate yearly progress in student performance among all student subgroups at the school. The reason for this conflicting dichotomy was the simple fact that educational fraud was going on at the school. Lopez said:

> They held kids out in the testing. They didn't test every kid. They did not test the special kids. They held out a huge subgroup of [English language learner] kids.

Among the special education students, Lopez said, "There are kids here who haven't been tested in three years." The federal law requires that a high percentage of students from subgroups like English language learners and special education take the state test, specifically to prevent schools from increasing their scores by keeping low-performing students from testing.

For this reason, Lopez said, "I love No Child Left Behind." He believes that "No Child Left Behind is the best law that ever happened for minority kids." It was the federal act and its adequate yearly progress requirement that caught the fraud.

> Like Watergate's Deep Throat, Lopez rips away the veneer of seeming success at his own school.

When he was hired as the principal, Lopez immediately asked why the school had not met the federal adequate yearly progress goals. He said that the school's governing board basically said, "What's that?" The board, he observes, had been basking in the lie that OCA was a great school, and became angry when he questioned the validity of the school's apparent accomplishments.

If OCA really was a failure, then what were the reasons for its poor performance? The reasons, it turns out, were many and started very early in the school's history. Lopez said, "In the rush to do everything differently from the public school system, they created a parent-involvement school." Parents would run the school, choose the administrators, and pick the curriculum.

It turned out that during the first years of operation, the parents could not settle on a good principal. In one year, for instance, four different individuals occupied the principal's office. Disputes between parents and the principals became so heated that the parents would change the locks to keep the principal out.

The school's governing board so micromanaged affairs that the principal was left with little authority. Lopez said that the previous principal would show up at 10 a.m. and be gone by 1 p.m. "There were too many cooks in the kitchen," observed Lopez, "so what you had was a school led by committee." The result was that it "created all kinds of issues among the staff with the kids."

Lopez went on to say, "After parental involvement they focused on culture. They focused on learning about Mexico and Mexican history, and learning Spanish — for a group of Mexican immigrant kids who probably speak Spanish better than the teacher."

Academic achievement, recalled Lopez, was "way down the list." The school did not have textbooks for 10 years. Lopez scornfully pointed out:

> The few books they did have — some math workbooks — the parents bought. They wouldn't even buy the books, they would make the parents buy the books. This was just a backwards place.

Because of the lack of textbooks, the school had no structured Language Arts program. Instead, English language arts was taught through social studies. Students would do a paper on, for example, Africa and that would count not only as their social studies, but as language arts as well. Yet Lopez observed that it was obvious from reading the writing that the children did not even know what a noun was.

> Disputes between parents and the principals became so heated that the parents would change the locks to keep the principal out.

The baleful reply from the school's leadership and teachers, according to Lopez, was the excuse that "these kids are English learners, they can't do that yet." "That was the whole issue with the textbooks," he concluded, "because these teachers felt that these kids couldn't do it."

Instead, the school focused on an extreme multicultural philosophy more in keeping with university ethnic studies departments than with the operations of a middle school. In fact, said Lopez, one key member of the school's governing board had a doctorate in ethnic studies. Another board member "had an MBA, but had no idea what was going on with the money. But all of a sudden she seemed to be this wizard about what's right for multicultural children."

The school's misguided multicultural emphasis manifested itself in a variety of ways. Before taking over as principal, Lopez visited OCA and in one classroom observed the children sitting in a circle. The teacher told Lopez, "we're sitting on the floor to get back to our Native American roots." The teacher, Lopez noted, "was German." According to Lopez, activities such as the "community" circles wasted valuable instructional time:

> They spent 45 minutes in community circles talking about problems; they spent 90 minutes in Spanish class — these kids are fluent in Spanish, they need to learn English; they spent 55 minutes in lunch; they spent another 30 minutes on breaks because these kids need breaks. . . . It was a party here.

Time was also lost through a monthly school dance. And staff development activities ate into instructional minutes. These activities, which included an all-expenses-paid week-long retreat to a Napa winery, did not produce anything worthwhile. Lopez said bluntly: "It was a sham. I think it's something that comes with this cooperative, creative leadership. And all the focus on this culture crap." Lopez said he is not at the school to teach culture; that is a job for parents. "My job," he said, " is to educate them."

The emphasis on bilingual education at OCA made no sense to Lopez. Talking to a Mexican-born member of the school's staff, he said: "'Let me ask you something. When you moved to the United States, did you come here and take Spanish classes?' He said, 'No, I took English.' And I said, 'Why are you teaching these kids Spanish?' He had no answer. So he said, 'Well, you can't change the charter because it's a document.'"

In short, activists used parental involvement as a cover to teach a particular ideology to the children. Lopez said: "On the very, very inner layer, what they really wanted to do was to pump out their ideology. They wanted the kids to be learning about native [culture]." And the children knew what was happening. Lopez observed: "The kids feel ripped off. They feel ripped off and they're angry."

One of the great ironies of this culture-based "education" is that immigrant families did not recognize the culture that was being force-fed to their children. Lopez said that at OCA, "They were teaching this other culture that families, especially Mexican families, are not familiar with." Because it was spiced with "liberal jargon," Lopez said that Mexican parents complained to him that "My kid said I can't discipline him," or "My kid is out and he said I don't have to listen to you anymore."

Lopez noted that contrary to the notions of the "progressive" culture

The teacher told Lopez, "We're sitting on the floor to get back to our Native American roots." The teacher, Lopez noted, "was German."

zealots, schooling in Mexico is very traditional and no-nonsense. According to Lopez:

> Mexico does a fine job of educating kids. The problem with Mexico is the poverty rate and the corruption. But you go to Mexico, you're in the same classroom from 8 to 5 o'clock. They don't give you lunch, they don't give you a break, they don't have recess. You take your lunch, you eat it quickly, and you go back to class and you learn. The reason they do this in Mexico is because they know these kids are going to drop out. They know that most kids in Mexico drop out because of realities — you've got to go to work. Their philosophy is to pump them full of education, of academics, while they've got them.

He noted: "There isn't all this quackery there is in the United States."

It comes as no surprise, given the culture-focused, anti-textbook mentality of the school, that there was also a strong bias against testing. Children at the school told him that tests "don't matter." He would respond by saying, "If tests don't matter, that means none of you will ever go to a university." His point is that "we have to measure ourselves."

Fiscal mismanagement was also a big problem. The school had operated under deficits. Further, Lopez explained: "At this school there was a 40-hour parental involvement [requirement], but parents never came. Instead they would pay $10 an hour for the 40 hours and they created this scheme where the money would be funneled to the principal." Also, Lopez said: "And it came out that the parents were paying money to get into the school. There wasn't a lottery. They would pay money."

Lopez blames some of the fiscal mismanagement problems on the teacher and administrator education system. He said: "I'm in my doctorate program and I've been hearing the same ol' crap since my B.A. It's about liberation. It's about the oppressed. I went through my whole master's program and nobody ever talked about the fiscal issues. What about how are we going to manage the money? Oh, don't worry about that, we first have to remember how this poor child has to overcome 'the man.'"

The school lunch program was also a joke. According to Lopez: "When I got here there was a taco truck parked in the middle of the play-

> One of the great ironies of this culture-based "education" is that immigrant families did not recognize the culture that was being force-fed to their children. Lopez said that at OCA, "They were teaching this other culture that families, especially Mexican families, are not familiar with."

ground. That was their lunch program. The taco truck would pull in from the back, and the teachers would be out there, with rap music blasting. This is at the school that was considered successful. It's an amazing thing when you see the numbers and then actually see the school."

The teachers at OCA were a huge part of the problem. They had bought into the school's program and were appalled that Lopez wanted to change direction. Just weeks after he was hired in June 2004, a meeting was held where teachers and some of their parent allies made a last-ditch stand to preserve the status quo. They ended up being unsuccessful, in part due to the fact that the majority of parents eventually came out to support Lopez. In July, Lopez fired the entire old crew at the school, not only teachers, but everyone from the secretaries to the janitors.

"I'm not in this business to create jobs for people or to create money," Lopez said, "I'm in it to run a good school because I believe in charter schools." He emphasized that "my sole focus is to run a solid charter school with low-income, minority kids."

Like some of the other principals interviewed for this book, Lopez blames misplaced idealism as the reason some charter schools lose sight of why they are in business. For example, he said that when he emphasizes high student achievement, he actually gets a negative reaction from some:

> When I talk like that with certain very liberal people, people who just care about everything but the kids, they get offended. They get offended because they're not about the kids, they're about their idealism. I had a board member tell me, "What are you doing — our kids don't need to go to college. Our kids can change this neighborhood from within." I said, "Excuse me, where do your kids go to school? Where do you live?"

The bottom line for Lopez is to improve the opportunities for the children at his school. Because they disagreed with his attitude and beliefs, and, even more, were surprised that his efforts started to truly raise student performance, the entire governing board stepped down. There is now a whole new board that governs the school and which agrees with Lopez that academics and student achievement are the school's priorities. As Lopez said, "It was a few months of hell, but it worked out."

Talk with Lopez and there is no doubt that OCA was one bad school. Yet a happy ending is being created. His new emphasis on academics and performance has started to bear fruit, which has impressed the California Charter School Association. Lopez said that the association's president, former Los Angeles school board president Caprice Young, has predicted that the school's test scores are going to go "through the roof."

Like Ben Chavis, Lopez does not coddle his students: "I'm very tough on these kids because the people I remember in school were the ones who were tough on me." He recalled, "They said, 'We're going to be on you because we know you can do it.'" Lopez has especially fond memories of Mr. Greenwood, his elementary school principal and a former football player for the Pittsburgh Steelers:

> He made me earn every grade, made me realize the path I was heading down, not by being this super nice guy, but by waking my ass up to reality. So I try to do that to these kids. We have kids here who have some serious potential, but they're caught up in this neighborhood thing. There are family issues that are going on. For them, I say, "I'm not going to help you at all with those things. I'm going to help you get smart, that's my job. That's what Mr. Greenwood would tell me. I can't go to your house and tell your mom to get along with your dad. I can't do that, I can't worry about what clothes you wear. I can make sure you get a good education."

It is noteworthy that as an undergraduate Lopez worked for the famed Hispanic high school calculus teacher Jaime Escalante. Lopez said that Escalante was "the most amazing teacher I ever saw." Escalante's low-income minority students achieved not only because of his teaching skills, "but because he demanded." "There was no democracy in his class,"

"And it came out that the parents were paying money to get into the school. There wasn't a lottery."

observed Lopez. According to Lopez, Escalante did not believe in parental involvement, he believed in work. It is no surprise that the only movie shown at OCA is *Stand and Deliver*, which tells the story of Escalante's teaching success.

To rectify the years of missteps at OCA, Lopez has purchased standards-aligned textbooks in every subject area and instituted test-taking skills classes. Also, he said, the school's focus has changed to reading and language arts, with 90 minutes allotted for instruction every day. Every teacher uses a scripted curriculum. "These kids need structure," observes Lopez. The school also brings in algebra tutors twice a week.

With only a 20-minute lunch period and no other breaks, the school day at OCA, which runs from 8:30 a.m. to 3 p.m., has more instructional minutes than at other schools. "I tell the kids," said Lopez, "what we're dealing with is an issue of time." He goes on: "It's not what they can do, it's about how we can be more efficient to create this product. The product is smart kids. So we have to maximize every minute we have."

The only remediation occurs in the summer. "That's when we catch 'em up," said Lopez, "but we don't water it down." The tutors refocus the lessons, but the expectation is for the children to produce and to be the best. Lopez said that the students are meeting this challenge.

Lopez has especially high hopes and expectations for his sixth graders since they have not been damaged by the mockery that passed for education at the school in previous years. He proudly noted that six of his sixth graders tested for the Center for Talented Youth at Johns Hopkins University. He said: "By the time they leave the eighth grade, they're going to be at the top of Oakland, I'm sure of that. It's because we got them smart and we're going to make them even smarter."

The school emphasizes a teacher-centered direct instruction approach. Under this method, said Lopez, "the teacher teaches and you focus on the teacher." The teachers use the textbooks as their instrument to get students where they need to be. "That's it," he said, "it's not rocket science."

Unlike the earlier era at the school when tests were scorned and derided, OCA now focuses a great deal on the various tests that students must take. For example, Lopez said:

> Our approach to the state test is the Big Game. All our talk here is about the championship game. This is the championship team. I'm the manager. The teachers are the coaches. The kids are the players. Our focus is the Big Game. We have a sign out there — it's counting down the days to the Big Game. I'm the one who led the class [on the discussion after] we watched *Stand and Deliver*, and I talked about the Big Game.

The new textbooks, better teaching methods, and high expectations are paying off. For instance, on the California English Language Development Test, which is given to English language learners to test English fluency, the school's population of 80 percent English language learners is now, according Lopez, scoring through the roof after only a summer and five months under the new instructional system. His satisfaction is tempered by the realization that the school's old regime wanted children to score low in order to get more federal Title III money. Lopez said: "To me it was like, no, I don't want that. You keep your Title III money, I want smart kids!"

Like at American Indian Public Charter School, Lopez is using the team concept to create an esprit de corps among his students. He said, "We make the weaker ones better, and we make the stronger become leaders — they're the captains for the team." Thus, an eighth grader may admonish a younger student with sagging pants by saying: "We don't do that here, pick your pants up." Students are now encouraging each other to "do your homework," "no cheating," or "you need to pay attention." Lopez observes that there is still culture at the school, but it is "a culture of excellence" and "a culture of expectation."

Like Ben Chavis, Lopez does not coddle his students: "I'm very tough on these kids because the people I remember in school were the ones who were tough on me."

Thus, an eighth grader may admonish a younger student with sagging pants by saying: "We don't do that here, pick your pants up."

Since OCA now uses the self-contained-classroom model that is used at American Indian, top-tier teachers are a must. After firing the school's previous faculty, he said he "hired the smartest teachers I could lay my hands on." Like Ben Chavis and Lisa Blair, he used Craigslist.com to find his teachers. He hired individuals with straight-A undergraduate grades from universities like Wesleyan, an honor student from UCLA, and a Math Olympian from China named Hai Yu Chen. Lopez said that Ms. Chen is the toughest teacher on his staff, but her students have responded:

> The kids believe in themselves now. They're working here until 4:30 p.m., just producing. They don't have time to mess around. They go home and they're doing their homework. They're just flying through this stuff. This is because she doesn't know anything else but to demand. She is not watered down with American schooling, the American education system. She didn't have a credential. She just entered her credential program. And I said, "Don't let that credential program ruin you."

Lopez emphasized, "I've made a point of not hiring credentialed teachers." He wants to have some time with the new teachers before they get their credentials so he can influence them. When his teachers enter their credentialing programs, Lopez said that their master's teachers come to visit the school. He is amazed that on all their visits not one of them has ever asked him about the textbooks or curricula used at the school. It is no wonder that he is singularly unimpressed by university schools of education: "We're going with the law school, the business school. I avoid the education programs because they're messed up. They're damaging and it filters down to the children. I don't want to do that at my school."

Given his success in transforming the teacher corps at OCA, it is unsurprising that Lopez said that the best thing about being a charter school is the fact that his school is not unionized and he can hire and fire at will. He said: "Everybody here can go at any time. It's like a business to me. I look at it as a business — my mom and pop store. If they're stealing from these kids, I'm going to fire them. That's one thing I enjoy."

Finally, as principal of a middle school, Lopez said, "The middle school years are the most essential time in these young people's lives." While state and local education officials are focusing on reforming high schools, Lopez contends that "middle school is the key."

When his teachers enter their credentialing programs, Lopez said that their master's teachers come to visit the school. He is amazed that on all their visits not one of them has ever asked him about the textbooks or curricula used at the school.

He cites Fremont High School, the school where most OCA students go after graduation. Fremont, he said, "has one of the highest dropout rates in California." Given the high potential of the students OCA received from its feeder elementary school, Lopez sets out the causal chain: "So we get them smart, we make them dumb, and then we make them drop out." But, he said confidently: "I'm not going to have that anymore. This school is going to be a totally different place."

WHAT STRUGGLING SCHOOLS HAVE TO SAY

We do not have flexibility in spending. Our budget is set because our teachers are members of the sponsoring district's bargaining unit. . . . [It] severely hampers our spending power.
— PRINCIPAL, ACADEMY CAREER EDUCATION CHARTER SCHOOL

IN ADDITION TO SENDING SURVEYS to improving charter schools, PRI sent surveys to lower-performing charters as well. Low performance was defined based on the inability of a charter to meet its state test-score improvement target in two years out of a three-year period, from 2001–02 to 2003–04. There were seven schools that fell into this category.

Out of the seven underachieving schools, only one school, the independent-study Academy for Career Education (ACE), returned the survey. ACE had a 2003-04 demographic of 70 percent White students and 13 percent Hispanic students. The comments from ACE's survey were interesting and shed some light on the problems facing this school.

The survey sent to the low-performing charter schools was nearly identical to the surveys sent to the highly improving schools. The exception was question number three, which was changed from asking which of a variety of factors explained the success of the school to instead asking which of a variety of factors are the most important to establish. In answer to this question, the principal of ACE, who has headed the school for six years, lists high student expectations, parental involvement, use of technology, curriculum, and small class size, in that order, as the criteria she wants to establish and maintain at her school.

It may be that it is harder to enforce a discipline policy in an independent-study setting. However, even if this is true, the bottom line is that ACA seems to be experiencing some level of student behavioral problems that may be disrupting the learning process.

In other words, she lists criteria that, in many ways, mirror the responses of the principals at the highly improving charters. Also, when it comes to hiring teachers, the principal prizes willingness to learn and ask questions, ability to work with others and be part of a team, experience with low-income or at-risk youth, and subject matter knowledge. The principals at the better charters also look for these traits.

Professional development at ACE is based on the state standards, individual teacher requests and the request, of the majority of staff, also criteria which are important to many principals at the highly improving charters. During classroom observations, the principal checks for understanding, examines the use of technology, and observes small group instruction.

The relationship between ACE and the local school district is rated as nearly excellent, although the need for better communication is noted. There is also a character education program and the state test results are used as diagnostic tools by teachers. Again, these are characteristics of better-performing charters.

If there are so many similarities between ACE's responses on the survey and the responses of highly improving charters, why has it been difficult for the school and its students to achieve at a higher level? Clues may be found in some of the short answers provided by ACE's principal.

The principal cited one major problem: "We do not have flexibility in spending." She blamed the fact that "our budget is set because our teachers are members of the sponsoring district's bargaining unit," which "severely hampers our spending power."

The school's lack of flexibility may mean that needed classroom materials cannot be purchased or that certain programs cannot be offered. In fact, ACE's leader estimates that her school spends 85 percent of its budget on personnel costs, which is higher than any of the estimates provided by the principals at the highly improving charter schools. Indeed, the 85 percent figure cited by the principal is 30 percentage points higher than the lowest figure, 55 percent, at non-union Reems.

As a result of her personnel costs, the ACE head said that only 5 percent of her budget is spent on curriculum, which is a quarter of the percentage spent at Reems and half the percentage spent at Vaughn, Montague, and Sixth Street Prep. Also, the school spends nothing, zero percent, on before-school, after-school, and summer-school supplemental instruction programs. In contrast, three of the better charters spend 10 percent of their budget on supplemental instruction, while another spends 7 percent.

Also, textbooks seem not to be used widely at the school. Instead, the school focuses on "individual tutoring sessions with an instructor where materials are given out based on individual need."

The principal did not answer Question #19, which asked: "Which reading materials that you use do the teachers find to be most useful?" It would be troubling if the reason for this non-response is that none of the materials have proven useful.

ACE's principal also did not respond to Question #16: "How would you describe the pedagogical methodology at your school?" Since the school is an independent-study school with instructors serving as tutors, it may be that each instructor has his or her own favored teaching method. However, given the connection between student performance and particular pedagogical techniques, it is worth noting that many of the highly improving charters use one or two proven methods.

Another potential problem area is discipline. At Reems, for example, student behavior was so bad that Lisa Blair had to attack that problem before she could make a dent in the school's academic challenges. All the principals at the highly improving charters indicated that their discipline policies were working and that there were few student behavioral problems at their schools. This calm allows learning to take place in the classroom.

"That's what happens at charter schools that are really unsuccessful. You've got all this ideology, with people on the board who think they can do a better job. They create these big ideas and they never show up or they never follow through, or it's just totally against what's going to work."

In contrast, the principal writes that ACE's discipline policy is only "somewhat" successful. As opposed to most of the principals at the highly improving charters who said that they used a consistent discipline policy from class to class, based on staff consensus, the principal said that because ACE is an independent-study school, discipline policy is "based on individual need, with a discipline framework used as a guide." It may be that it is harder to enforce a discipline policy in an independent-study setting. However, even if this is true, the bottom line is that ACE seems to be experiencing some level of student behavioral problems that may be disrupting the learning process.

Dolores Huerta

One poorly performing charter school that failed to send back a survey was Dolores Huerta charter school in Oakland. Although the school did not respond, it is still possible to get some insight into the school's problems. Jorge Lopez, the new principal at Oakland Charter Academy, was a teacher and, for a brief time, the principal at Huerta. Besides discussing the failings at OCA, he also explained the reasons for the low performance at his previous school.

Lopez spared no words in calling the Huerta governing board "a bunch of wackos." The board, according to Lopez, is motivated by the same Latino-culture-focused ideology that used to be the guiding philosophy at OCA. For example, Spanish language is emphasized, with the result that students score poorly on English exams.

Also, Lopez said that Huerta is obsessed with parental involvement, to the point that it is the parents who do the evaluations of the teachers.

Lopez bluntly observed: "That's the biggest crock I've ever heard. With due respect, my parents couldn't do it. My mom has a first grade education, and she's going to evaluate a teacher? So the principal there [is just a figurehead]."

The Huerta governing board also micromanages school affairs. Lopez said that it is difficult for a principal at the school to do anything significant without running it by the board. Further, he pointed out that the decisions made by the board are based on ideology, not empirical evidence: "That's what happens at charter schools that are really unsuccessful. You've got all this ideology, with people on the board who think they can do a better job. They create these big ideas and they never show up or they never follow through, or it's just totally against what's going to work."

It is also noteworthy that like Lisa Blair at Reems, Lopez had a bad experience with the School Futures, the charter management organization. He said: "They were terrible managers — they created all sorts of fighting within the community. They promised everything and gave nothing." It was after a fight with School Futures that he describes as "ugly" that Lopez left Huerta.

CHAPTER ELEVEN

THE DOS AND DON'TS

Gone are the days when it was cause for celebration if a charter, any charter, was created and approved. With around 500 charter schools in California, the emphasis must shift from quantity to quality.

FOR THOSE WHO PAINT CHARTER SCHOOLS with a broad brush and see them only as a single category, this book amply demonstrates that not all charter schools are alike, nor are they created equal. Not only are improving charter schools different from those that are not improving, the good charters also differ than each other. Yet, along with these differences there are also some commonalities that can inform charter school organizers, parents, and school boards regarding which models of charter schools work and which do not.

As was noted at the beginning of this book, the very definition of charter schools implies that they will be different, at least to some extent, from the regular public schools and also from each other. For instance, while it may have been thought that all the highly improving charter schools would not be part of the local teachers' union collective bargaining agreement, that turned out not to be the case. Some of the schools voluntarily agreed to abide by the union contract, while others did not.

Not all the schools used the same curricula or textbook series. There were variations in teaching methods and classroom structure. American Indian Public Charter School used a self-contained classroom model, while most other schools did not. Schools dealt differently with the student behavioral problems that plagued them early in their histories. Some schools felt that parental involvement was vitally important, while others believed the exact opposite.

If all the highly improving charter schools were totally different from each other, it would be difficult to decide which characteristics or practices at the schools should be replicated at new charters. However, despite a number of differences, there is a set of underlying similarities that should serve as a guide for the charter movement.

- **Good management and consistent, stable leadership**
  A successful school's leadership focuses on student achievement, cost efficiency, and fiscal responsibility and accountability. Virtually all of the principals had headed their schools for five years or more. Many also had a business background, were entrepreneurial in their approach to management and operations, and concentrated on getting the most bang for the school's buck.

- **Academic rather than non-academic goals, with high expectations for students and staff**
  Principals want their students to have the highest test scores in the district or to hit certain high-performing benchmarks. Regardless of the student's socioeconomic background, the school expects that students can achieve the high goals set for them.

- **Rigorous standards-based curricula, with acknowledgement of the importance of textbooks**
  The state's academic content standards guide instruction, which means that the curricula must be aligned with the standards. Students should have textbooks to use both in the classroom and at home.

- **Hiring of smart teachers based on top academic records, not on regular teaching credentials or years of experience**
  A number of the charter schools use unorthodox sources such as Craigslist.com to find smart teaching candidates. With an effective school model, principals want teachers who are intelligent and are open-minded enough to buy into and implement the model.

- **Collaborative professional development for teachers**
  Grade-level teams of teachers meet regularly to analyze student

data, plan for interventions, and design instruction. To best improve teacher performance, teachers at a school must get together to discuss what is working and what is not in their classrooms.

- **A clear emphasis, to students and parents, on the importance of testing**
  Students are assessed often, with classroom and state test scores used as diagnostic tools to spot student weaknesses, inform interventions, and influence design of instruction.

- **Test score data used as a check against grade inflation**
  Grades need to reflect true student performance, not a teacher's subjective impulses. Although grading may pick up certain student performance factors missed by a test, testing data can help validate the credibility of student grades.

- **Use of teaching methods that are empirically proven to improve student performance**
  The research shows that some teaching methods are better than others when it comes to increasing student performance. In order to achieve the school's academic goals, it is critical that the teaching methods be effective. If teachers are given flexibility to choose teaching methods, then their choice must be tied to the requirement that it leads to higher student achievement.

- **Frequent classroom visits by the principal to ensure high-quality teaching**
  Principals have to know what is going on in the classroom. The school may have a good academic plan, good curricula, and high expectations, but all these things may be undercut by poor execution in the classroom. Frequent classroom visits by the principal will ensure that deficiencies will be corrected quickly.

- **Rigorous teacher evaluations and real consequences, such as termination, for poor performance**
  Objective criteria should be established to measure teacher performance. Plans for improvement should be part of any evaluation, but the teacher

should be given a short time frame to improve his or her performance. Failure to improve must result in termination, since the victims of poor teaching are the children.

These factors common to the highly improving charter schools are absent from those charters that are struggling. For their part, charters that are having academic problems seem to share a number of the following characteristics.

- **Infighting among stakeholders**
  This can include organizers, board members, administrators, staff, and parents. When there is disharmony among stakeholders, the focus centers on the disagreements rather than on educating children. Valuable time and energy is wasted.

- **Revolving door leadership, resulting in a lack of stability and consistency**
  Good principals need to be in their job for a long enough time to implement the school's vision and plan. Constantly changing principals means that instead of needed continuity, leadership will be by fits and starts. This often results in the school's goals remaining unmet.

- **Governing board micromanagement that deprives the principal of decision-making authority**
  The governing board should be responsible for large policy decisions, but not the day-to-day educational operations. The failure to understand this demarcation will cause operational dysfunction since the principal will not be able to make independent decisions and the board is not around in most instances to make those decisions.

- **Principal and other school leaders with little management and/or business experience**
  This situation leads to fiscal inefficiency and irresponsibility, as well as the lack of an accountability system to catch mismanagement. A charter school is a working entity, just like a business, with employees, budgets, and fiscal choices. Leaders who do not know how to run such an organization will end up mismanaging it, squandering money, and jeopardizing the continued existence of the school.

- **A focus on the non-academic ideals of the school's adults rather than on the academic needs and achievement of students**
  This includes teachers who are not committed to academic learning, or who are not subject to rigorous evaluation with consequences for poor performance. Charter schools are not ideological playthings for their organizers, administrators, and staff. Charter schools are granted freedoms in order to improve student achievement, not to satisfy the whims of adults.

- **Use of unrealistic and/or unproven philosophy of teaching or learning**
  Teaching and learning philosophies must be judged on whether they improve student performance, not on how satisfying they are to teachers and other adults at the school.

- **Failure to use charter freedoms and flexibilities to break the status quo public school mold**
  It is important for charter school leaders to think outside the box both in terms of academics, as long as it improves student performance, and in business operations.

- **Bias against testing students and pushing them to perform up to the level of the state's rigorous academic content standards**
  Regardless of one's ideological position on testing, the failure to understand that a charter school is accountable for the achievement of its students, which means performance on tests aligned to the state standards, will likely result in low student achievement and the revocation of the school's charter.

- **Discouraging perceived low-performing students from taking the state standardized tests**
  It is appalling that some charters try to mask their incompetence by preventing certain students from taking the state tests.

- **Weak curricula, with no textbooks provided to students**
  Curricula, especially in the core subjects, should be chosen for their rigor and alignment with the state standards, not on non-academic grounds.

In this age of accountability, charter schools have to demonstrate that they are performing. Gone are the days when it was cause for celebration if a charter, any charter, was created and approved. With around 500 charter schools in California, the emphasis must shift from quantity to quality. In order for existing and future charter schools to achieve that desired level of quality, it is imperative that schools be aware of successful models and eschew those practices guaranteed to cause failure.

As this book shows, there are charter schools that are implementing innovative and effective measures to raise the performance of their students. If others follow their example, the strength of the charter movement will grow. The beneficiaries of that strength and growth will be California's children, many of whom are currently suffering in regular public schools that are not only poorly performing, but are often dangerous. If California is to remain a national and international economic powerhouse, then charter schools and the children they educate will have to meet the quality challenge.

OTHER CHOICE OPTIONS FACING CALIFORNIA

CALIFORNIA HAS BEEN ON THE FOREFRONT of the charter school movement. The state's charter law is now a dozen years old and there are more charter schools in California than anywhere else in the nation. Yet as advanced as California may be when it comes to charters, it must be pointed out that the state lags when it comes to other forms of parental choice.

Indeed, it must be remembered that the idea of charter schools is based on the view that parents should have more choices in where to send their children to school. Charter schools were an alternative to the traditional public schools, which were often providing an inadequate education. Further, the competition offered by charter schools could spur the other schools to improve their performance.

If the concepts of choice and competition as embodied in charter schools were admirable, then the same concepts should be encouraged when they take other forms. There are currently a number of different parental-choice options that have been instituted in other parts of the country which California policymakers would do well to investigate and perhaps bring to the state.

The most discussed and debated choice alternative is, of course, vouchers or opportunity scholarships. Parents may use this government-funded aid to pay for private school tuition. Types of existing programs in the U.S. include: means-tested vouchers that allowed families meeting usually low-income specifications to be eligible to participate; accountability vouchers, which grant aid to those families whose children attend failing traditional

> If the concepts of choice and competition as embodied in charter schools were admirable, then the same concepts should be encouraged when they take other forms.

public schools; and special education vouchers, which give aid to families of children with specific needs.

The Milwaukee voucher program is the nation's longest-running means-tested voucher program, established in 1990–91. Children are eligible to receive a voucher of up to nearly $6,000 if their family earns less than 17.5 percent of the federal poverty level. Just over 13,000 students use the vouchers at more than 100 private schools. Because the Milwaukee program has been in existence the longest, the research on its effectiveness is the most extensive.

There have been several studies done by researchers from Harvard University. One found that after four years in the program, students achieved a six-percentile gain in reading and an 11-percentile gain in math. Another study found that public schools most exposed to the competition from the voucher responded by increasing the math scores of their own students. A Princeton University study found that after four years in the program, students achieved an eight-percentile gain in math. For a summary of the research on the Milwaukee voucher program and other city programs, see "The ABCs of School Choice," published by the Milton and Friedman Foundation, February 2004.

The voucher program in Cleveland is smaller than the one in Milwaukee, serving about 5,000 students who use the vouchers at 45 private schools. The voucher amount can be up to $3,000. Indiana University researchers have found that voucher-receiving students perform equal to or better than their public school peers.

It is worth noting that in California, the nonpartisan Legislative Analyst's Office (LAO), in its 1998—99 state budget analysis, recommended: "We think the idea of vouchers has sufficient merit that the Legislature should sponsor a demonstration program as a way to understand the costs and benefits of the concept. A demonstration program would select a small number of schools where students would be given the opportunity to apply for a voucher."

Since the time of the LAO's recommendation, there has been new research showing that vouchers have a positive effect on student achievement. Thus, if it made sense to have at least a pilot voucher program in 1998–99, then it makes even more sense today, especially given the continued poor performance of schools at the lowest end of the state's Academic Performance Index.

Under a pilot voucher program, at least some parents would have more choices of where to send their children to school. Also, like the state's class size reduction program, a research component could be attached to the pilot voucher to determine if the program was increasing the achievement of students. For its part, the LAO recommended that "As part of the program, researchers could address a number of important questions: What choices do voucher-holding students have? Do they fare better than similar students who remain at the [public] school? How does the [public] school respond to this type of competition? Do special education students seek and use vouchers?"

There is growing support for a voucher option among influential members of the state. For example, in 2003, California Senator Dianne Feinstein, a Democrat, displayed great political courage by coming out strongly in favor of a federally funded voucher for students in Washington, D.C. According to Feinstein: "Based on the substantial amount of money pumped into the schools and the resultant test scores, I do not believe that money alone is going to solve the problem. This is why I believe the [District of Columbia] should be allowed to try this pilot — particularly for the sake of its low-income students."

Feinstein, who credits her own schooling at a Catholic high school for her success in life, concludes that the issue isn't about "ideology or political correctness," rather: "It is about providing a new opportunity for good education, which is the key to success. Unless a youngster has learned the fundamentals of education, he or she will find it extremely difficult when older to find work in the competitive marketplace."

Feinstein's support for the Washington, D.C. voucher proposal was a critical element in its eventual approval by Congress. Given that the scores of many California children are every bit as bad as those of the children in D.C., it seems logical that some type of pilot voucher program, as proposed by the LAO, should be tried. Indeed, if it is a moral and civil right to give parents in Washington the ability to choose the best education for their children, then why shouldn't California parents be allowed that same right?

Another type of program gives vouchers to students who attend consistently failing public schools. Florida enacted an accountability voucher program in 1999. Under the program, children are eligible if they attend a public school that receives an "F" grade two years out of a four-year period from Florida's Department of Education. The average voucher is just over $4,200 and is used by around 700 children.

The Florida program could be replicated easily in California using the state's school accountability system. Under this system, schools that fail to improve are already subject to a number of sanctions, including replacement of the principal, re-negotiation of union contracts, closure, or being turned into a charter school. It would be a simple matter to add an accountability voucher to the list.

This would be a great incentive for these schools to improve. In Florida, low-performing schools that faced the prospect of vouchers showed significant improvement on the state's reading and math tests.

Florida also has a voucher program aimed at students with disabilities. Parents who are unhappy with their children's public school can receive a voucher to be used at a private school or another public school. The median voucher amount is around $6,000. About 14,000 students use the voucher to attend more than 600 private schools. As opposed to the dissatisfaction they had with their children's public schools, parental satisfaction with the private schools is above 90 percent.

In addition to vouchers, the other major type of school-choice program involves either tax credits or tax deductions. Tax-credit programs usually give dollar-for-dollar refunds for approved expenses that families incur at private schools, while tax-deduction programs usually lower taxable income. There are also tax-deduction programs that offer individuals or businesses the ability to make tax-deductible donations to organizations that give out scholarships to children to attend private schools.

These tax-credit and tax-deduction programs are often easier to implement since all that is required are changes in the state's tax code. This is simpler than having the state create and oversee a voucher program that determines eligibility and sends voucher checks to parents. For example, Minnesota's tax-deduction program was started 50 years ago. Parents receive a state tax deduction for tuition at private schools. Parents may receive a deduction of up to $1,625 per child in grades K–6 and $2,500 per child in grades 7–12.

Minnesota also has a school-choice tax credit that was instituted in 1997. The tax credit is aimed at lower-earning families and gives them a refundable credit of up to $1,000 per child, and a maximum of $2,000 per family, for non-tuition expenses at private schools such as books, supplies, and services.

In 2002, approximately 218,000 Minnesota families used the school-choice tax deduction and saved nearly $250 million on their state taxes. In the same year, more than 56,000 families claimed the tax credit resulting in $14.5 million being distributed.

California opponents of the school-choice tax-deduction and tax-credit programs will argue that given the state's budget deficits, it would be imprudent to enact programs that reduce state revenues. The state, however, spends $10,000 per student in state, federal, and local tax dollars. Families with children in the public schools that decide to take advantage of a tax deduction/tax credit, which would be smaller than the amount the public schools spend per child, in order to send their children to private schools, would end up saving the state money. Research on the Florida tax-credit program shows this to be the case.

In addition to ease of implementation, tax-deduction and tax-credit programs are much less likely to be challenged in court than voucher programs. The Florida accountability voucher program, for instance, has been mired in the state's courts for years. Issues involving so-called Blaine amendments that prevent the distribution of state funds to religious organizations such as parochial schools have often been the cause of these legal challenges. California has a Blaine amendment. In contrast, the U.S. Supreme Court has upheld the constitutionality of Minnesota's tax-deduction program and no legal challenge has been made against the tax-credit program. No future legal action is anticipated against either of the programs.

It should be noted that Pennsylvania has enacted a tax-credit program aimed at preschool-age children, while Florida has enacted a preschool voucher program. Under the Pennsylvania program, businesses receive tax credits for the contributions they make to non-profit preschool scholarship organizations approved by the state. Businesses receive a 100 percent credit for the first $10,000 they contribute, plus up to a 90 percent credit for any contributions up to $100,000.

The organizations then award scholarships to eligible families that have three-year-old and four-year-old children. Eligibility is based on family income, which has to be $50,000 or less, with a $10,000 allowance for each dependent. Families can use the scholarships to send their children to any public, private, independent, or religious preschool program.

Florida's preschool voucher program, which is scheduled to begin operation in 2005–06, gives a scholarship of up to $2,500 to families with four-year-olds that can be used to send the child to a private preschool. Parents may also send their children to public preschools.

The Pennsylvania and Florida programs are less intrusive and less expensive than the universal-preschool ballot initiative proposed in California by former actor Rob Reiner. The Reiner initiative will appear on the state's June 2006 ballot and would result in most children attending government-run preschools. Extremely conservative estimates of the cost of Reiner's initiative hover around $6,000 per child and $2.3 billion in total, but these figures do not include key costs such as facilities and transportation.

Before making the decision to support the Reiner initiative, Californians should become informed about the school-choice preschool alternatives in places like Pennsylvania and Florida.

The point is that California should not settle for just being a leader in charter schools. There is a constellation of parental choice options that are being tried and tested in other parts of the country. With leaders in the California mainstream, such as Senator Feinstein, coming out in favor of vouchers and given the relative ease of enacting tax-deduction or tax-credit programs, state policymakers should broaden their school-choice sights. They should enact reforms that will provide more children with the opportunity to have a better education.

NOTE ON METHODOLOGY

WHEREAS TRADITIONAL PUBLIC SCHOOLS tend to have similar characteristics because of the centralized decision-making of school district officials, charter schools are an entirely different story. Charter schools, by definition, differ not only from traditional public schools, but also from each other by virtue of the freedom to chart their own curricular, instructional, and philosophical courses. Studies that lump all charter schools together fail to recognize this critical fact. It makes little sense to combine the performances of a direct instruction charter school that emphasizes core academic subjects and a charter school that focuses on progressive pedagogies, cultural heritage issues, and students constructing their own base of knowledge.

Furthermore, a charter school that has made great strides in improving the achievement of previously poorly performing students may have more interesting lessons to teach policymakers than an equally ranked school whose performance has remained static for years.

Thus, rather than looking at aggregate level data we analyze the performance of individual charter schools to find out why particular schools are performing the way they are. The information gained from such an examination would help to indicate successful educational models that low-performing charter and traditional public schools could emulate. Also, low-performing charter schools may be using education models and practices that contribute to student underachievement and which should then be used either extremely cautiously or not at all by new charters.

Because a key argument in favor of charter schools is that they help improve the performance of students, especially low-socioeconomic students, and charter proponents emphasize the importance of looking at this improvement over time, this book gathers information about both continuously improving charter schools in California and charters not showing sustained improvement. Schools in both categories were chosen based on their scores on California's Academic Performance Index (API) over a three-year period from 2001–02 to 2003–04. These scores were then compared to the school's growth target.

A school's API score is based on the performance of students on California's standardized tests that are aligned with the state's academic content standards. Every school is given an annual growth target, that is, an improvement benchmark score that it needs to meet in order to avoid potential consequences under California's school accountability system. The unfortunate reality, however, is that based on the way growth target scores are calculated, it takes relatively little improvement by a school to meet the new benchmark. Indeed, James Lanich, president of the California Business for Educational Excellence and an expert on testing data, points out:

> Under [the state Academic Performance Index], schools could be meeting their "growth" targets while at the same time, achievement gaps among individual students could be widening. Additionally, the state API growth target is calculated in such a way that in many cases it will take students an unacceptable 30 years to reach proficiency at the rate of growth acceptable under the California API system.

Thus, simply meeting a growth target score may not indicate that quality practices are being implemented at a charter school, or at any school for that matter.

In consultation with researchers at the California Charter School Association, the quality-driven state organization of charter schools, we decided that to be counted as a continuously improving charter school, a school would have to meet not only its state-prescribed growth target, but would also have to exceed that target by at least seven points. This added improvement target would both assure that a school was doing better than the minimum expected by the state and was likely employing quality practices. It would not, however, be an unrealistically high goal given the often challenging student populations enrolled at charter schools. The school would have to exceed the growth target every year during the three-year period.

To be labeled a non-improving charter school, a school had to fail to meet its state-prescribed growth target two years out of the three-year period and have a ranking of five or below on the API's one-to-ten ranking system. The ranking system is based on the scores on the state's standardized tests. The state views a rank of five or below as low performing. Because the growth targets are low, a struggling school may still occasionally meet the target. But if a school fails to meet the low targets several times over the period, then it may be assumed that the school may be experiencing problems.

Based on these criteria, we examined the test score data on the state's charter schools. Since many are new, there were not enough years of data on them to categorize them. Of those that did have the requisite years of data, many met the state's annual growth targets but did not meet the added improvement criteria in one or more years. Others failed to meet the state growth target in one year, but met the targets the majority of the years. It turns out that the universe of charter schools that exceeded the targets every year over the time period and those that failed to meet the targets a majority of the years was relatively small. There were 10 continuously improving schools and seven non-improving schools.

To find out what was going on, survey instruments were first sent to the principals at each school. The surveys asked about the practices employed at the school, probing subjects such as the factors that lead to school success, teacher quality, and classroom discipline policies. Of the 10 surveys sent out to the continuously improving charter schools, eight were returned. One of the 10, Oakland Charter Academy, turned out to be a special case and the school is profiled in the section on poor-performing charters. Of the seven surveys sent out to the non-improving schools, one was returned. Tabulations were then made of the responses.

In addition, we made site visits to the continuously improving schools, interviewed the principals, and observed classroom instruction. We asked the principals to discuss the reasons for their school's improvements, the challenges that had to be overcome, how charter freedoms were used, and their observations of why failing charter schools performed poorly. The principals were open, forthcoming, and had strong opinions about what worked and what did not in improving student achievement.

SCHOOL SURVEYS AND RESULTS

THE SURVEY SENT TO PRINCIPALS at highly improving charter schools cover a wide range of issues that are meant to explore why these schools are doing well. Issues include the experience of the principal, factors contributing to school academic success, budget and spending flexibility, teacher hiring policies, collective bargaining participation, professional development activities, relationship with the local school district, curriculum and instructional choices, and discipline and parental involvement policies. To glean information on these topics, the survey includes questions that ask principals to rank various factors in order of importance and others that require a short explanation. The questionnaire can be found in the appendix.

Looking at the experience of the principals, it turns out that most have been at their school for at least five years. Of the seven schools that returned surveys, six out of seven principals had been the principal at their current school for five years or longer, with four having more than 10 years at the school. Two had 15 years at their school. The only principal with five years or less in experience had four years. The average years spent in their current job was 9.7 years.

That the principals had been at their current posts for a lengthy period of time is significant. Stability of leadership is an important component in building a successful school. Joe Lucente, the principal at Fenton Charter School, said that good schools need good teachers, but he points out "you still have to have leadership." In looking at poor-performing charter schools, one of the common negatives is a revolving door in the principal's office. With multiple principals in a single year or over a short period of years, a charter school cannot hope to implement long-term strategies and visions. However, with a single competent leader at the helm, a charter school can focus on long-term improvement goals.

Stable leadership is a necessary but not sufficient ingredient for a successful school. Excellent curricula, effective teaching methods, and a variety of other factors impact the achievement of students at a school. When asked to rank the top five factors (among 15 listed) behind the academic success of their school, we find some interesting clustering of answers among the principals.

For instance, six out of the seven surveyed listed high expectations for students among their top five factors, with four listing it as either their first or second most important success element. Although it might be taken for granted that most schools have high expectations for their students, it is actually far from the case. The bigotry of low expectations is alive and well, unfortunately, at many regular public schools and, as we have seen in this book, at some charter schools as well.

Also seen as important by many of the principals was having teachers knowledgeable in both subject matter and pedagogy. This factor was listed by six of seven principals and was ranked first or second by four of them. That these principals recognize the importance of subject matter competence and effective teaching methods demonstrates that they understand what empirical research has shown: Student achievement is strongly tied to teachers who understand their subject fields and who employ instructional methods that are proven to raise student performance.

Assessing students to gauge their progress and to discover their weaknesses is a common-sense tool, but one that is not always favored by many anti-testing elements in the education establishment. However, showing that they favor what works over fashionable opinion, five of the seven principals listed ongoing formative assessment as one of their top five factors, with one listing it as the second most important.

Once a student is found to have weaknesses in one or more areas, based on assessment results, then schools can target interventions or supplemental instruction to correct the student's deficiencies. This logical follow-up step after assessment is listed by four out of the seven principals as one of their top five factors.

Realizing that high-quality teachers are critical to a school's success means making sure that good teachers become even better. This improvement process is assisted by both staff development and by common planning time for teachers, both of which were listed by three out of seven principals as among their top five factors. As seen in their comments, the principals interviewed for this book have found that techniques such as grade-level planning by teams of teachers have proven to be key elements in raising teacher effectiveness and student learning.

Receiving one vote each were curriculum, grade-level standards, character education, parental involvement, technology use, school mission, and professional governance/professional acceptance of responsibility. It is interesting that small class size also received just one vote given the program's popularity among politicians and education special interests, such as the teacher unions. Small school size received no votes despite the fact that a number of the schools did have relatively small student populations.

When given six budget areas and asked to give a percentage breakdown of where the money goes, the responses were fairly uniform. Not surprisingly, personnel was estimated to eat up anywhere from 55 percent to more than 80 percent of a school's budget. Facilities costs were responsible for up to 3 percent to 10 percent; nearly 3 percent to 20 percent for curriculum; zero to 10 percent for staff development; zero to 5 percent for parental involvement; and 1 to 10 percent for supplemental instruction.

When asked how they used the budget flexibility that comes from being a charter school, answers varied. The principal at American Indian Public Charter School said, "I know when to spend the money and when not to waste money." He uses his funds to employ "smart people and pay them well." At Sixth Street Prep, the budget focuses on the school's plan, and carry-over is used to meet long-term goals such as technology and computer-based instruction. The principal at Fenton Avenue Charter School said: "We try to get as much 'cluck for the buck.' Better, faster, cheaper!" At Bowling Green Charter School, flexibility is used to reduce pupil-teacher ratio, add support staff such as nurses and counselors, and improve facilities.

Hiring policies are one traditional area of charter flexibility. When asked which of 13 factors were the top four criteria that guided the hiring of teachers, most of the principals looked for the ability to work with others and be part of a team. Six out of seven chose this factor and three said it was their top priority while two more listed it as their second. Given that many of these schools have a specific philosophy and way of doing things, it is not surprising that principals want their teachers to support the school's goals and be part of a team that aims at reaching those goals.

Of course, children are the focal point of schools so it is natural that four out of seven principals said that "love of children" is an important hiring factor, with one principal listing it as the top factor and another picking it second. Principals also want their teachers to have strong classroom management skills. Four of the principals listed this choice.

It is interesting that three principals chose the "other" category, with the principal at Fenton listing it as the number one choice and filling in the blank with "smart/strong work ethic." The principal at American Indian rated "other" as his second factor and wrote in teachers' "grades in college." The principal at Bowling Green also gave "other" a number two and wrote down "charter spirit."

During our interviews, many of the principals voiced concern that prospective teachers have often been indoctrinated with certain ideologies at university schools of education. There was a sense that many of these teachers wanted to teach their way, not the school's way. Thus, it follows that willingness to learn and ask questions was listed by three out of seven principals. The same ratio of principals also listed knowledge and willingness to implement state standards as one of their top four factors.

Two out of seven principals chose teachers' subject matter knowledge, but it was the first choice of one and the second choice of the other. Similarly, two out seven chose pedagogical knowledge, with one of the two listing it as the top choice.

One very interesting finding of the survey was the lack of interest expressed by principals in the experience of teachers. Experience with specific student groups, such as low-income students, received one vote. Years of experience, the lack of which is often cited as a reason for poor teacher quality at low-performing schools, was not listed by a single principal as a factor in their teacher hiring. Specific grade-level experience also received no votes. Neither did specific extra-curricular background and experience. The message seems clear: These charter school principals do not subscribe to the conventional wisdom that experience equals quality.

Given the high proportion of English language learners in many of these charter schools, it is perhaps initially surprising that no principal listed the ability of a teacher to speak two languages as an important hiring factor. However, in the profiles in this book, most of the principals say that they use full English immersion to transition English language learners to English fluency. With English immersion, as opposed to bilingual education, it is less important that teachers have a second-language skill.

One of the perceived handcuffs on teacher hiring-and-firing flexibility is the teacher union contract. These contracts usually contain seniority clauses, burdensome due process measures, and other hand-tying provisions. Charter schools have the freedom to either voluntarily abide by the collective bargaining agreement or to be a non-union school. Among the seven highly improving charter schools, four are not part of the union contract. However, it is noteworthy that three are.

There is a diversity of opinion as to the impact of the collective bargaining agreement. The principal at Vaughn New Century Learning Center said, "Handcuffs off, performance in," while the principal at Reems says: "Performance is high. School practices are flexible and can be adjusted to meet needs of staff and students." On the other hand, in the profiles, a couple of the principals at charters that do abide by the union contract say that they have not been affected adversely by the agreement. On the flip side, though, the principal at Bowling Green, which abides by the union pact, said that the agreement "negatively impacts staffing, especially when [an] unwanted teacher is surplused into the school."

In order to make good teachers better, schools should have effective professional development activities. However, teacher professional development in California is a mish-mash of programs of unproven worth. When given a choice of six factors that could focus professional development at their school, principals were asked to choose their top three. Six out of seven listed the state academic content standards as a professional development guide, with two listing it as their first choice and two listing it as their second. Also, six out of seven said that the needs of the majority of their teachers affected professional development activities, with two making it their first choice and three as their second. A slightly different factor, "Request of the majority of staff," was chosen by four out of seven principals.

Two out of seven principals allowed the individual need of a teacher to guide professional development, and both these principals listed it as their number one choice. One principal listed the individual request of the teacher, while another chose "other" and wrote in "student need."

To determine the effectiveness of teacher professional development, many schools used student performance as a common gauge. Comments included: "Teacher evaluation and improved academic achievement" at Fenton; "Classroom visits, assessment data, and grade-level planning" at Sixth Street Prep; "Student performance" at Bowling Green; and "Through feedback, demonstration, and student work" at Reems.

A charter school raison d'être is that it will use its freedoms and flexibilities to be different from regular public schools. The principals were asked how their schools differed from their traditional public-school counterparts. The principal at Reems wrote: "We are not bound by bureaucracy. We're able to maintain consistency, not harassed by whims of the district." Other interesting comments: "Maintain a team of effective teachers" from the principal at Vaughn; "Fiscal and curricular independence — can include art and music" from the principal at Bowling Green; and "Using lots of technology" from Sixth Street Prep's principal.

While stories of strained relations between charter schools and local school districts are widespread, it is interesting that most of the principals rate their relations with their district as good to excellent. Only one principal rated the relationship as fair. Many of the comments reflected this good relationship, although the principal at Vaughn did write: "If all eligible funding sources came directly from the state [to the charter school], bypassing [the Los Angeles Unified School District], we will not have to fight for our fair share."

When asked about the school's preferred pedagogical method, the answers ranged from direct instruction to focusing on English proficiency to a variety of strategies. The principals clarify these answers in the earlier school profiles sections of this book.

In the interviews, a number of the principals said that their observations in the classroom were critically important. What were they looking for? Asked to choose their top three factors from a set of 12, six out of seven principals chose "differentiated instruction for multiple abilities," although five out of the six listed it as their third choice. Four out of seven chose "checking for understanding," with three listing it as their second choice.

Three out of seven looked for a "clear objective," with one principal listing it as number one and the others listing it number two. Two out seven wanted to see "students on task," and both listed this factor as number one. Two out of seven also focused on "classroom management" and on "teacher modeling of instructional objectives," with each receiving a number one and number two ranking. One principal wanted "knowledge and implementation of the state standards," and listed it as the top factor.

Not all the principals were specific in naming the reading and math texts used at the schools. For those that did, Open Court for reading and Harcourt for math were listed by several. A number of other texts were also named. Reasons given for choosing the texts ranged from their alignment to the state standards to the fact that the texts were research-based to piloting and selection by the school's teachers.

California's standards-aligned tests are often the target of criticism by anti-testing elements in the education establishment. However, when asked what schoolwide actions are taken as a result of the state tests, most of the principals indicate that the test results are put to great use. Comments include: "focus on training teachers" at American Indian; "results are analyzed at all levels for planning" at Montague; "analyzed by grade level; compare individual student scores" at Fenton; "analyze and modify [school] plan based on results" at Sixth Street Prep; and "teach test-taking strategies, insure that grade-level skills are taught, train teachers" at Reems.

As the profiles describe, a number of the schools had major student behavioral problems in their early years, which is likely the reason that five out of the seven schools implement some type of character education program. Five out of seven also said that their discipline policy is "consistent from class to class, based on staff consensus," rather than "varies from class to class, based on the teacher." Two out of seven say that it is a combination of these two policies. All say that their discipline policies have been successful.

Most of the schools listed parental involvement as middling to high. One school listed it as low. In the profiles, it is interesting to find out the differing opinions as to the importance of parental involvement, with some principals believing it is extremely important while others believe the exact opposite.

Asked an open-ended question as to any other important factor at their school, Vaughn's principal cited consistent leadership; the principal at Sixth Street Prep said "high expectations and incentives to achieve;" and Fenton's principal wrote, "Everyone works hard and with one purpose: the success of our students."

Survey for High-Performing Charter Schools

Pacific Research Institute
Survey for Charter School Principals

Name of School: _____

Name of Principal: _____

Experience

1. How long have you been the principal of this school?

_____ Years

2. How many years were you the principal of other schools?

_____ Years

Academic Success

3. Choose and prioritize: What are the top <u>five</u> criteria that make your school academically successful? (1 = most important)

_____	a.	High academic expectations of students by teachers
_____	b.	Teachers knowledgeable in both subject matter and pedagogy
_____	c.	Curriculum
_____	d.	Supplemental instruction for targeted students (intervention)
_____	e.	Character education program
_____	f.	Staff development
_____	g.	Ongoing formative assessment
_____	h.	Parental involvement
_____	i.	Grade level curriculum standards
_____	j	Small school size
_____	k.	Small class size
_____	l.	Use of technology
_____	m.	School mission
_____	n.	Common planning time for teachers
_____	o.	Other (*Please specify*) _____

4. **How have you ensured that the five criteria you selected above are in place in your school?**

Budget
5. **What percent of the school's budget do you spend on:**
_____ a. Facilities
_____ b. Curriculum
_____ c. Staff development
_____ d. Parental involvement activities
_____ e. Personnel
_____ f. Supplemental instruction (Before school/ After school/ Summer programs)

6. **(a) How do you use the flexibility in spending that you have as a charter school?**
   (b) Are there any areas in which you have no flexibility in spending that you would like improved?

Hiring
7. **Choose and prioritize: What are the top <u>four</u> qualities you look for in a prospective teacher?**
   (1 = most important)

_____ a. Strong skills in classroom management
_____ b. Willingness to learn and ask questions
_____ c. Love of children
_____ d. Subject matter knowledge
_____ e. Pedagogical knowledge
_____ f. Specific grade level experience
_____ g. Specific extra-curricular background and experience
_____ h. Years of experience
_____ i. Experience with a specific student group (such as low-income or rural)
_____ j. Ability to speak two languages
_____ k. Ability to work with others and be a part of a team.
_____ l. Knowledge and willingness to implement state standards
_____ m. Other (Please specify) _____

8. **How do you determine whether the teachers you are interviewing have the qualities you are seeking?**

Collective Bargaining
9. **Has the school voluntarily decided to abide by the district collective bargaining agreement?**

_____ No
_____ Yes

10. **How has this decision affected school practices and performance?**

Professional Development
11. **Choose and prioritize: What are the top <u>three</u> ways you determine the focus of professional development activities?**
(1 = most important)

_____ a.   Individual teacher need
_____ b.   Individual teacher request
_____ c.   Focus on state standards
_____ d.   Need of majority of staff
_____ e.   Request of majority of staff
_____ f.   Other (please specify)_____

12. **How do you evaluate the effectiveness of the professional development you provide?**

Use of Charter Freedom
13. **(a) How does your school differ from other public schools in the district?**
   (B) What is working particularly well?

Relationship with the District
14. **On a scale of one to six, how would you describe your relationship with the school district?**

Poor   Excellent
1   2   3   4   5   6

15. **How do you think your relationship with the district could be improved?**

Curriculum and Instruction

16. **How would you describe the pedagogical methodology at your school?**

17. **What are the top <u>three</u> things that you look for when you are observing a teacher in the classroom?** (1 = most important)

_____ a. Clear objective
_____ b. Students on task
_____ c. Teacher-led whole group instruction
_____ d. Small group instruction
_____ e. Classroom management
_____ f. Use of learning centers
_____ g. Teacher modeling of instructional objectives
_____ h. Use of technology
_____ i. Checking for understanding
_____ j. Differentiated instruction for multiple abilities
_____ k. Knowledge and implementation of state standards.
_____ l. Other (Please specify) _____

18. **(a) What textbooks and supplemental materials do you use to teach reading and math?**
    (b) Why did you choose these materials?

19. **Which of the reading materials that you use do teachers find to be the most useful?**

20. **Do you implement a character education program in your school? If so, please describe:**

21. **What schoolwide actions do you take as a result of state-level tests?**

Discipline
22. Which best describes your classroom discipline policy: (select one)

_____ a.   Varies from class to class, based on teacher
_____ b.   Consistent from class to class, based on staff consensus
_____ c.   Other (please specify) _____

23. Do you think your discipline policy is successful? Why or why not?

Parental Involvement
24. On a scale of 1 to 6, how would you describe parental involvement at your school?

Low   High
1   2   3   4   5   6

25. Is there anything else you'd like to add about your school?

SURVEY FOR LOW-PERFORMING CHARTER SCHOOLS

PACIFIC RESEARCH INSTITUTE
SURVEY FOR CHARTER SCHOOL PRINCIPALS

Name of School: _____

Name of Principal: _____

Experience
1. How long have you been the principal of this school?

_____ Years

2. How many years were you the principal of other schools?

_____ Years

Academic Success
3. Choose and prioritize: What are the top five criteria that you think are the most important to establish and maintain at your school? (1 = most important, 5 = least important)

_____ a. High student expectations
_____ b. Teachers knowledgeable in both subject matter and pedagogy
_____ c. Curriculum
_____ d. Supplemental instruction for targeted students (intervention)
_____ e. Character education
_____ f. Staff development
_____ g. Ongoing formative assessment
_____ h. Parental involvement
_____ i. Grade level curriculum standards
_____ j Small school size
_____ k. Small class size
_____ l. Use of technology
_____ m. Other (Please specify) _____

4. How do you ensure that the five criteria you selected above are in place in your school?

Budget
5. What percent of the school's budget do you spend on:
_____ a. Facilities
_____ b. Curriculum
_____ c. Staff development
_____ d. Parental involvement activities
_____ e. Personnel
_____ f. Before school/After school/ Summer programs

6. How do you use the flexibility in spending that you have as a charter school?

Hiring
7. Choose and prioritize: What are the top four qualities you look for in a prospective teacher? (1 = most important)

_____ a. Strong skills in classroom management
_____ b. Willingness to learn and ask questions
_____ c. Love of children
_____ d. Subject matter knowledge
_____ e. Pedagogical knowledge
_____ f. Specific grade level experience
_____ g. Specific extra-curricular background and experience
_____ h. Years of experience
_____ i. Experience with low-income or at-risk youth
_____ j   Ability to speak two languages
_____ k. Ability to work with others and be a part of a team
_____ l. Knowledge and willingness to implement state standards
_____ m. Other (Please specify) _____

8. How do you determine that the teachers you are interviewing have the qualities you are seeking?

Collective Bargaining
9. Has the school voluntarily decided to abide by the district collective bargaining agreement?
_____ No
_____ Yes

10. How has this decision affected school practices and performance?

Professional Development
11. Choose and prioritize: What are the top three ways you determine the focus of professional development activities? (1 = most important)

_____ a.   Individual teacher need
_____ b.   Individual teacher request
_____ c.   Focus on state standards
_____ d.   Need of majority of staff
_____ e.   Request of majority of staff
_____ f.   Other (please specify)_____

12. How do you determine the effectiveness of the professional development you provide?

Use of Charter Freedom
13. How does your school differ from other public schools in the district?

Relationship with the District
14. Please rank your relationship with the school district on a scale of one to six

Poor   Excellent
1   2   3   4   5   6

15. How do you think your relationship with the district could be improved?

Curriculum and Instruction
16. How would you describe the pedagogical methodology at your school?

17. What are the top three things that you look for when you are observing a teacher in the classroom?

_____ a.   Clear objective
_____ b.   Students on task
_____ c.   Teacher-led whole group instruction
_____ d.   Small group instruction
_____ e.   Classroom management
_____ f.   Use of learning centers
_____ g.   Teacher modeling of instructional objectives
_____ h.   Use of technology
_____ i.   Checking for understanding
_____ j.   Differentiated instruction for multiple abilities
_____ k.   Knowledge and implementation of state standards
_____ l.   Other (Please specify) _____

18. What textbooks and supplemental materials do you use to teach reading and math? Why did you choose these materials?

19. Which of the reading materials that you use do the teachers find to be the most useful?

20. Do you implement a character education program in your school? If so, please describe:

21. What do you do with the results of state-level tests?

Discipline
22. Which best describes your classroom discipline policy? (select one)

_____ a.   Varies from class to class, based on teacher
_____ b.   Consistent from class to class, based on staff consensus
_____ c.   Other (please specify) _____

23. Do you think your discipline policy is successful? Why or why not?

Parental Involvement
24. On a scale of 1 to 6, how would you describe parental involvement at your school?

Low   High
1   2   3   4   5   6

25. Is there anything else you'd like to add about your school?

SURVEY RESULTS MATRIX

		American Indian	Vaughn	Montague	Fenton (Sumida)	Sixth Street	Bowling Green	E.C. Reems Academy	Oakland Charter	Academy for Career Education
1	Years at current school?	5	15	12	12	4	15	5	1	6
2	Years at other schools?	4	6	9	0	0	0.75	0	3	0
3.a	High academic expectations of students by teachers	3	1	2	1	1		x	1	1
3.b	Teachers knowledgeable in both subject matter and pedagogy	2	2	1	2	4		x	4	
3.c	Curriculum		5	3					3	4
3.d	Supplemental instruction for targeted students (intervention)	5		4				x	5	
3.e	Character education program		3		4		5			
3.f	Staff development	4		5			3			
3.g	Ongoing formative assessment		4			2	4	x		
3.h	Parental involvement								2	2
3.i	Grade level curriculum standards					3				
3.j	Small school size									
3.k	Small class size									5
3.l	Use of technology	1			3			x		3
3.m	School mission									
3.n	Common planning time for teachers				5	5	2			
3.o	Other	internal accountability system		closely monitored by councils	emphasize at all opportunities	focus on these issue in all mtgs. long range plans submitted around monthly benchmarks.	1 (professional goverance, professional acceptance of responsibility) built into process of school. Are part of routines.	regular mtgs between teachers and administrators to review progress; principal personally review student work samples; formal and informal evaluations	changed curriculum and increased minutes	self-assessment, staff meeting
	How have you ensured that the five components in #3 are in place?									
4										

		American Indian	Vaughn	Montague	Fenton (Sumida)	Sixth Street	Bowling Green	E.C. Reems Academy	Oakland Charter	Academy for Career Education
5.a	facilities budget	10%	10%	3%	4.2%	5%		5%	10%	0%
5.b	curriculum budget	5%	10%	11%	2.8%	10%		20%	10%	5%
5.c	staff development budget	0%	10%	5%	2.8%	8%		5%	5%	5%
5.d	parental involvement (scale of 1-6)	0%	3%	3%	1.5%	1%		5%	0%	5%
5.e	personnel	73%	60%	68%	83.0%	75%		55%	60%	85%
5.f	supplemental instr.	10%	7%	10%	3.0%	1%		10%	15%	0%
	How do you use the flexibility in spending?	I focus on employing smart people and paying them well.	Freely deploy fiscal resources.	Not a program-driven budget	involve all teachers, don't use traditional district routine	Budget based on school plan. Use carryover to met long-term goals.	Reducing teacher/ student ratio; Additional support staff; improving facilities.	Spending is all geared to providing the best learning opportunity for students	Some staff members are not full-time	No flexibility in spending, budget is set because teachers are in district union
6.a	Are there areas you would like improved?	n/a	Spec. Ed.			no	no	no		
6.b										
7.a	Strong skills in classroom management	4	3	4			3	4		
7.b	Willingness to learn and ask questions				4	2		10		1
7.c	Love of children	1	2		3	3		1		
7.d	Subject matter knowledge			1				2		
7.e	Pedagogical knowledge		4					7		
7.f	Specific grade level experience							5		5
7.g	Specific extra-curricular background and experience							11		
7.h	Years of experience							9		
7.i	Experience with a specific student group (such as low-income or rural)					5		3		3
7.j	Ability to speak two languages		1					12		
7.k	Ability to work with others and be a part of a team	3		2	2	1	1	8	4	2
7.l	Knowledge and willingness to implement state standards						4	6	1	
7.m	Other	2		3	1	4	2		2,3	

	American Indian	Vaughn	Montague	Fenton (Sumida)	Sixth Street	Bowling Green	E.C. Reems Academy	Oakland Charter	Academy for Career Education
8 How do you determine whether the teachers you are interviewing have the qualities you are seeking?	Designed a job listing	references/demo lesson	demo lesson	Interview and observation process. Honest with teachers about school's expectations	clearly defined culture which is reflected in questions asked.	check references; demo lessons	interview to find out if candidate is truly inspired; demo teaching, peer interview, hrs of rec, transcripts	recruit at top Liberal Arts colleges	questions and responses
9 Does the school abide by the district's collective bargaining agreement?	yes	no	yes	no	yes	yes	no	no	yes
10 How has the decision (#9) affected the school?	handcuffs off, performance in			positive professional environment	Decide by staff consensus	negatively impacts staffing, esp. when unwanted teacher is surplused into the school.	performance is high; school practice is flexible to adjust to student needs	high pay for staff	severely hampered our spending power and autonomy
11.a individual need		1				1			
11.b individual request		2						2	2
11.c state standards	1	3	2	3	3	2	1	1	1
11.d needs of majority	2		1	1	2	3	2	2	
11.e request of majority	3		3	2			3		3
11.f other					1 (student need)			3 (director choice)	
12 How does school determine effectiveness of professional development?	research by university		based on need	teacher eval and improved academic achievement	classroom visits; assessment data; grade level planning	student performance	Feedback, demonstrations, and student work.	use services used by other proven charter schools	have not provided any

		American Indian	Vaughn	Montague	Fenton (Sumida)	Sixth Street	Bowling Green	E.C. Reems Academy	Oakland Charter	Academy for Career Education
13.a	How does school differ from district schools?	smart people/provide support	maintain a team of effective teachers	decisions are easily made	everyone is a life-long learner	only Option I CSR school; using lots of technology	fiscal and curricular independence; can include Art and Music	Not bound by bureaucracy. Good ideas are enforceable. Able to maintain consistency, not harassed by whims of a district	small, self-contained, uniforms, etc.	independent study; focus on career education
13.b	What is working well?	structured academics		curriculum can be easily adjusted			independence; curriculum independence; site-based decision making		all of it	
14	How is relationship w/district?	6	4	6	3	6	4	5	5	5
15	How could it be improved?	excellent relationship	state should give eligible funding directly to school	excellent relationship	would be helpful if district saw school as a partner	Pleased with current relationship.	Better educating central office staff	Positive relationship with district. Could benefit more from a better report time table	Hiring own Spec. Ed. personnel	Better communication
16	School's pedagogical method?	traditional	lots of LEP students, therefore focus is on language proficiency	direction instruction because it is research-based	standards-based curriculum with technology	technology enhanced DI; daily skill review	eclectic	hand-on; connect real life experience to curriculum, assess and use assessment to do planning	rigorous academics. Strong emphasis on reading	
17.a	Clear objective	2	2			1			3	
17.b	Students on task	1		1						
17.c	Teacher-led whole group instruction									
17.d	Small group instruction									3
17.e	Classroom management						1	2	2	
17.f	Use of learning centers									
17.g	Teacher modeling of instructional objectives					2		1		
17.h	Use of technology		3			3				
17.i	Checking for understanding	3	3	2	2		2		2	2
17.j	Differentiated instruction for multiple abilities	3	1	3	3		3	3		1
17.k	Knowledge and implementation of state standards				1				1	

	American Indian	Vaughn	Montague	Fenton (Sumida)	Sixth Street	Bowling Green	E.C. Reems Academy	Oakland Charter	Academy for Career Education
17.1 Other — reading and math texts	Holt Literature/ math Concepts	state adopted texts	Open Court, Saxon	Open Court/ Harcourt 200	Houghton Mifflin (R&M) Making Meaning; Destination Success; A/R; STAR Reader; Accelerated Math	Varies by each of six departments	Open Court (K-5); McGraw Hill High Point Reading (6-8); Hampton Brown OPEN BOOK (K-8); computer aided program	Harcourt, McDougall Littell, Prentice Hall Algebra 1	individual tutoring; materials given out based on individual need
18.a Why did you chose those texts?		aligned to standards	research-based and contribution to language dev.	piloted and selected by teachers			Harcourt (K-6)	aligned to standards & proven track record	
18.b What is the most useful reading material?	Holt Literature		Open Court and AR	Open Court	Making Meaning		Open Court (K-5) and HighPoint Reading. These provide solid foundation as reflected in CST/CAT6 scores	Language Arts Handbook (Harcourt)	
19 Do you implement a character ed program?	no	no	Core Virtues	Conflict and Anti Drug programs called Second Step and Too Good For Drugs	Premier Agendas and Character Connections.	Focus on Life Skills. Developed by Susan Kovalik.	Resiliency in education program focusing on: curriculum, teacher induction/retention, parent support, student projects	no	Yes. During pre-employment training skills training
20									
21 What schoolwide action do you take as a result of state-level tests?	focus on training teachers using structured academic program.	periodic block testing to monitor quarterly progress.	results are analyzed at all levels for planning.	analyzed by grade level; compare ind. student scores	analyze and modify plan based on results. Conduct ongoing formative assessments with monthly benchmarks.	Not much	teach test taking strategies; train teachers and require regular classroom testing;	focus on reading/LA. Increased daily instructional minutes. / many changes	Give them to teacher who works with the same group of students from year to year.

	American Indian	Vaughn	Montague	Fenton (Sumida)	Sixth Street	Bowling Green	E.C. Reems Academy	Oakland Charter	Academy for Career Education
22 Which best describes your discipline policy?	b (varies class to class)	c (both a and b) School discipline plan with some flexibility	b (varies class to class)	b (varies class to class)	b (varies class to class)	b (varies class to class)	c (both a and b) School discipline plan with some flexibility	b (varies class to class)	c (other) Independent study
23 Is your discipline policy successful?	yes, reduction in suspensions, higher time on task.	yes	consistent, clearly understood by students and positive	yes, school is calm and children rarely fight or argue.	yes, discipline begins with establishing routines and procedures in the classroom and that they are engaged in learning.	yes, as manifested by student and staff behavior.	Yes, schoolwide policies and classroom policies, also behavior management plans	yes. We create a no excuses atmosphere	somewhat
24 What is your parental involvement? (scale of 1–6)	1	6	6	4	6	2	4	2	6
25 Anything else?	oldest/one of the first conversion charters in the country. Consistent leadership		"see attached"	everyone works hard and with one purpose: the success of our students.	high expectations and incentives to achieve.			many changes this year	

A SCHOOL TO WATCH

College Ready Academy
Los Angeles, California

A STONE'S THROW FROM THE UNIVERSITY OF SOUTHERN CALIFORNIA campus in South Central Los Angeles sits College Ready Academy (CRA) charter school. But while the men and women of Troy stroll into beautiful, modern brick buildings, CRA is located in an aging one-building facility that could stand a bit of updating. Like many of the other schools described in this book, however, modest walls may mask the high-quality learning within.

The principal of CRA is Howard Lappin, a husky, gray-haired man who is taking on the challenge of leading a new charter high school after a legendary career at Foshay Junior High School, later Foshay Learning Center. When he took over Foshay in 1989, the school, whose students were all minority and mostly low income, was listed as one of the 31 lowest achieving in the Los Angeles Unified School District.

By the end of the 1990s, Lappin had completely turned Foshay around to the point where the school was recognized not only as one of the 10 best in Los Angeles, but was also named by *Newsweek* as one of the best schools in the country. For his efforts, Lappin was praised as an education "hero" by *Reader's Digest* and then California governor Pete Wilson, and he was named California's principal of the year.

CRA, Lappin's new school, is in an area where all the surrounding high schools have large student populations of more than 2,000 and are ranked in the bottom decile on the state's Academic Performance Index. Thus, CRA is an important alternative for parents in an area where the other public high schools are failing.

CRA is a small school with several hundred students, all of whom are Hispanic or African American. More than 90 percent of the students are on the federal free or reduced lunch program.

The school's philosophy is to prepare previously underachieving students with the skills, experiences, and knowledge to enter college. Given that Lappin succeeded in getting 70 percent of his students at Foshay to go to college, CRA's philosophy fits Lappin's like a glove. He said that he expects 100 percent of his students at CRA to graduate and go to college. From the moment they enter the school, students are told repeatedly that they are going to college, and this mantra is supplemented by the college pennants that adorn the school.

CRA is part of the Alliance of College-Ready Public Schools (ACRPS), an independent non-profit charter management organization chaired by well-known Los Angeles businessman and charter advocate Frank Baxter. ACRPS plans to build at least 20 high-performance, small K–8 and high schools in Los Angeles over the next five years. All the schools will use research-based best practices to prepare all students for college.

Although the school was only opened in August 2004, there has already been some marked improvement. In November 2004, the school worked with the Los Angeles school district to administer an internal language arts assessment. Only six percent of CRA's students were found to be proficient, while another 30 percent were approaching proficiency. In March 2005, a second language arts assessment was given and 25 percent of students scored at proficiency, while 38 percent were approaching proficiency.

One of the key reasons for the quick improvement in student achievement has been the school's focus on the state's rigorous academic content standards. Lappin insists on standards-based teaching. Teachers must show what standards they are emphasizing. Grades cannot be given based only on whether students show up or simply complete an assignment. Rather, grades must signify that students are meeting the standards.

Classroom materials must be linked to the standards as well. The teachers at CRA know the standards. But the key, says Lappin, is translating this knowledge into a standards-based instructional program in the classroom, while holding students accountable for the standards.

There are no elective courses at CRA. Most courses are core college prep that satisfy the University of California/California State University requirements. Remedial classes are the only electives. For instance, while a student may be taking algebra, the course replacing his elective could be basic math. Lappin says that this mixing of courses has been very effective.

In addition, like American Indian Public Charter School, CRA will use a looping model in which a student will stay with the same teacher in a subject field for his or her years at the school. Thus, students will have the same English teacher, the same math teacher, and the same social studies teacher during their time at CRA. Lappin observes that this will allow teachers to know their students and vice versa.

In a looping system, teachers have to be of excellent quality. Lappin hires teachers based on their knowledge of the standards plus their enthusiasm and belief in students' ability to learn and achieve. Like many of the principals at highly improving charters, Lappin said: "I'm not a big believer that having a credential is the be-all and end-all. I think that having a credential protects the union." He said that having a credential does not guarantee high quality. CRA is not part of the local teachers' union collective bargaining agreement and teachers are on a year-to-year contract. Lappin said that he strives to involve teachers in the decision-making process.

CRA tests students regularly. Lappin would like to test them monthly in order to see how they are doing and integrate those results into the lesson planning. He wants teachers to see where students are and figure out how they can get them to where they should be. He is a great believer in value-added testing, which collects student test data over time and gives a projection of how much test scores should improve from year to year. Teachers, says Lappin, should be held accountable if students do not improve during the school year. Students need to show a year's worth of growth after spending a year in the classroom.

Also, like other good charters, CRA has a longer school day. Classes start at 7:45 a.m. and end at 4:15 p.m. More time means more instruction and better results.

Lappin subscribes to the broken window theory, which says that in order to promote safety one must deal with the little infractions so as to deter the larger ones. His students are in uniform and he cultivates a culture of discipline: "My reputation is such that we don't put up with anything." Many of the parents send their children to CRA because it is a safe learning environment.

Lappin said, "There is no magic bullet. We all know what to do," he points out, "we just need the courage to do it."

A CHARTER SCHOOL RESOURCE GUIDE
FOR PARENTS

California Charter School Association
P.O. Box 811610
Los Angeles, CA 90017
(213) 244-1446
www.charterassociation.org
info@charterassociation.org

California Department of Education Charter Schools Office
School Fiscal Services Division
1430 N Street, Suite 3800
Sacramento, CA 95814
(916) 445-6761
www.cde.ca.gov/sp/cs/
tsun@cde.ca.gov

National Association of Charter School Authorizers
1125 Duke Street
Alexandria, VA 22314
(703) 683-9701
www.charterauthorizers.org

United States Department of Education
Office of Innovation and Improvement
400 Maryland Avenue, SW
Washington, DC 20202
(202) 260-1882
www.ed.gov/offices/OII/
dean.kern@ed.gov

Charter School Leadership Council
1090 Vermont Avenue, NW, Suite 800
Washington, DC 20005
www.charterschoolleadershipcouncil.org
info@cslc.org

U.S. Charter Schools
P.O. Box 66483, NW
Washington, D.C. 20035
(202) 463-7151
www.uscharterschools.org
andy@cslc.org

National Charter Schools Institute
2520 South University Park Drive, Suite Box 11
Mount Pleasant, MI 48858
www.nationalcharterschools.org
info@nationalcharterschools.org

Center for Education Reform
1001 Connecticut Avenue, NW, Suite 204
Washington, D.C. 20036
www.edreform.com
cer@edreform.com

INDEX

ABOUT THE AUTHORS

Lance T. Izumi is Senior Fellow in California Studies and Director of Education Studies at the Pacific Research Institute for Public Policy (PRI). He is the author of several major PRI studies, including "Putting Education to the Test: A Value-Added Model for California" (2004), the "California Education Report Card: Index of Leading Education Indicators" (1997, 2000, and 2003 editions), "Developing and Implementing Academic Standards" (1999), "Facing the Classroom Challenge: Teacher Quality and Teacher Training in California's Schools of Education" (2001), and "They Have Overcome: High-Poverty, High-Performing Schools in California" (2002).

In 2004, Governor Arnold Schwarzenegger appointed Mr. Izumi as a member of the Board of Governors of the California Community Colleges. In 2003, United States Secretary of Education Rod Paige appointed Mr. Izumi to the Teacher Assistance Corps, a task force of experts assigned to review state teacher quality plans as they relate to the federal No Child Left Behind Act. Mr. Izumi is a member of the California Postsecondary Education Commission. He also served as a member of the Professional Development Working Group of the California Legislature's Joint Committee to Develop a Master Plan for Education.

Mr. Izumi is the co-editor of two books: *School Reform: The Critical Issues* (Hoover Institution Press and Pacific Research Institute, 2001) and *Teacher Quality* (Hoover Institution Press and Pacific Research Institute, 2002). He is the chapter co-author of "Fixing Failing Schools in California" in *Within Our Reach: How America Can Educate Every Child* (Rowman & Littlefield, 2005) and "State Accountability Systems" in *School Accountability* (Hoover Institution Press, 2002).

Mr. Izumi served as chief speechwriter and director of writing and research for California governor George Deukmejian. He also served in the Reagan administration as speechwriter to United States Attorney General Edwin Meese III.

Mr. Izumi received his master's degree in political science from the University of California at Davis and his juris doctorate from the University of Southern California School of Law. He received his bachelor's degree in economics and history from the University of California at Los Angeles.

Xiaochin Claire Yan is a public policy fellow in education studies at the Pacific Research Institute. Ms. Yan has written on issues of education reform for a wide range of California newspapers, including the *Orange County Register, Los Angeles Daily News, San Francisco Examiner, Sacramento Union, Riverside Press-Enterprise, Silicon Valley Business Journal*, and *San Francisco Business Times*.

Before joining PRI, she was an editor at Regnery Publishing, a politics/current affairs publishing house in Washington, D.C. She has also worked at the editorial page of the *Wall Street Journal* in Asia, based in Hong Kong. Ms. Yan was a Collegiate Network journalism fellow and a contributing editor to *Choosing the Right College: A Guide to America's Colleges* (ISI Books, 2003).

Ms. Yan is a Los Angeles native and a graduate of Princeton University, with a degree in politics and international relations.

ABOUT THE PACIFIC RESEARCH INSTITUTE

The Pacific Research Institute champions freedom, opportunity, and personal responsibility by advancing free market policy solutions. It provides practical solutions for the policy issues that impact the daily lives of all Americans. It demonstrates why the free market is more effective than the government at providing the important results we all seek—good schools, quality health care, a clean environment, and economic growth.

Founded in 1979 and based in San Francisco, PRI is a non-profit, non-partisan organization supported by private contributions. Its activities include publications, public events, media commentary, community leadership, legislative testimony, and academic outreach.

Education Studies

PRI works to restore to all parents the basic right to choose the best educational opportunities for their children. Through research and grassroots outreach, PRI promotes parental choice in education, high academic standards, teacher quality, charter schools, and school finance reform.

Business and Economic Studies

PRI shows how the entrepreneurial spirit—the engine of economic growth and opportunity—is stifled by onerous taxes and regulations. It advances policy reforms that promote a robust economy, consumer choice, and innovation.

Health Care Studies

PRI demonstrates why a single-payer, Canadian model would be detrimental to the health care of all Americans. It proposes market-based reforms that would improve affordability, access, quality, and consumer choice.

Technology Studies

PRI advances policies to defend individual liberty, foster high-tech growth and innovation, and limit regulation.

Environmental Studies

PRI reveals the dramatic and long-term trend towards a cleaner, healthier environment. It also examines and promotes the essential ingredients for abundant resources and environmental quality property rights, markets, local actions, and private initiative.